# Called to Follow

Journeys in John's Gospel

# Called to Follow

Journeys in John's Gospel

&

Martha Ellen Stortz

CASCADE *Books* • Eugene, Oregon

CALLED TO FOLLOW
Journeys in John's Gospel

Cascade Books
An Imprint of Wipf and Stock Publishers
199 W. 8th Ave., Suite 3
Eugene, OR 97401

www.wipfandstock.com

PAPERBACK ISBN: 978-1-62032-574-2
HARDCOVER ISBN: 978-1-4982-8823-1
EBOOK ISBN: 978-1-4982-4105-2

*Cataloguing-in-Publication data:*

Names: Stortz, Martha Ellen.
Title: Called to follow : journeys in John's Gospel / Martha Ellen Stortz.
Description: Eugene, OR: Cascade Books, 2017 | Includes bibliographical references.
Identifiers: ISBN 978-1-62032-574-2 (paperback) | ISBN 978-1-4982-8823-1 (hardcover) | ISBN 978-1-4982-4105-2 (ebook)
Subjects: LCSH: 1. Bible, John. | 2. Discipleship. | I. Title.
Classification: BS2617 .S67 2017 (print) | BS2617 (ebook)

Manufactured in the U.S.A.                    JANUARY 6, 2017

*To two fellow travelers*

*Rosa Catherine Stortz, beloved sister*
*(1954–2011)*

*Margaret Louise Ward Stortz, beloved mother*
*(1924–2013)*

# Table of Contents

# Introduction

SEVERAL YEARS AGO I was invited to write an extended Bible study. Here's how the conversation went.

"You know I'm not a biblical scholar." My training is in Christian theology and ethics, which means I know enough Latin, Hebrew, and Greek to get myself in trouble, but participles don't keep me awake at night.

"Yup," came the reply. "That's why we're asking you."

"What's the topic?"

"Pretty much anything you want," the editor said. "You know our audience. You know about discipleship. Talk about discipleship to our audience."

I did know the audience. The readers talked back. Committed Christians and seekers, they hated authors who hid behind jargon, and they knew when someone was condescending to them. They taught me how to write simply without dumbing it down.

I didn't know about discipleship of Jesus, though—at least not as much as I wanted to. I could produce generic definitions. "Disciples" follow something or someone, and it could be a fashion trend, a style of humor, a talk show host, or a celebrity. "Discipleship" pointed to a lifestyle visible in a series of practices. Over time and in community, these practices train disciples in a certain way of life.

Disciples of Bruce Springsteen order in advance every new album. Disciples of Dan Savage download podcasts. Discipleship in the lost world of *Downton Abbey* includes ritual watching of every episode, often dressed in period costumes and drinking period beverages. I knew who disciples were; I knew what discipleship was.

But what difference did it all make? How did discipleship of Jesus work—and work on disciples? Those questions interested me, as a citizen, as a theologian, as an ethicist.

I consider myself a disciple of Jesus, despite the snappy reply I made to a friend who asked if I were a practicing Christian. "No. I got it right the first time."

I knew then, though, and I know now: I need all the practice I can get. The request gave me a chance to get more. I offered to write on the beatitudes in Matthew's gospel.

"Beatitude" is a fancy word for blessing. In Matthew's gospel, Jesus begins the first sermon in his public ministry with a word of blessing. "*Blessed* are the poor in spirit . . . ; *blessed* are those who mourn . . . ; *blessed* are the meek . . . ." (Matt 5:3ff.) These inaugural blessings promise a reversal of fortune to people whom conventional wisdom regarded as cursed. Jesus' blessing begins that transformation.

Then, in the same Gospel, Jesus concludes the last sermon in his public ministry with more blessing. This time he addresses it to "you that are *blessed* . . ." (Matt 25:34). It's not a coincidence.

The people whom Jesus blessed in the beginning of his ministry become empowered to bless others. They feed the sick; they give drink to the hungry; they clothe the naked. That's how discipleship works in this Gospel. The argument for discipleship in Matthew's gospel is graciously simple: the blessed become a blessing.

Shortly after I sent off the manuscript on Matthew, I was asked to speak on John's gospel. The invitation was an opportunity for a deeper look at discipleship. By this time, I was convinced that each one of the Gospels defines "disciple" differently. Each one makes a distinctive argument for discipleship. In Matthew, as I'd found, blessed disciples become a blessing to others. In Luke-Acts, the Spirit does the heavy lifting. Mark's disciples remain clueless about who Jesus really is, while the demons and outsiders see him clearly as the "Son of God." But what about John's gospel? In this most chatty of the Gospels, encounters with vivid characters interrupt Jesus' long discourses.

Who was the "disciple" in this account? How did discipleship work? What was the argument for discipleship in John's gospel?

Here's what I found when I attempted to address those questions.

John's Jesus was a man on the move. His feet were itchy, but his GPS seemed off. He set his face toward Jerusalem but didn't take the most direct route there. The Gospel telegraphs this restlessness early on. In the opening chapters, Jesus arrives on the scene as an adult and in transit. He walks and talks like one of the late great characters from *West Wing*.

At first, disciples were dazzled. "Where are you staying?" (John 1:38) They expect a street address; they get an invitation instead: "Come and see" (John 1:39). They came; they saw; they couldn't let Jesus out of their sight.

After his initial recruitment efforts in Jerusalem, Jesus abruptly changes course and heads into Galilee. There, Jesus expands the ranks with another invitation, equally compelling, frustratingly vague: "Follow me" (John 1:43). No destination is given, as in "Follow me to Capernaum." Or "Follow me as far as the Sea of Tiberias." No one knows where Jesus is headed; they know only they have to go with him.

Later in the Gospel, a road-weary Thomas explodes in frustration: "We don't know where you're going." If he hopes Jesus will respond with the name of a place they all might recognize, he's disappointed. Jesus answers: "I AM the way . . ." (John 14:6). What "way" is that?!

Jesus couldn't even stay in his grave. In three days, he eludes death, escapes the tomb, and appears to Mary Magdalene and then to the disciples in a locked room. Finally, he shows up along the Sea of Tiberias to cook everyone breakfast. After the meal, he engages Peter in a long conversation that concludes with the words that started the whole journey in the first place: "Follow me" (John 21:19). Then he departs from his followers for good, without

3

leaving them any directions. For the road ahead, they have only the call, "Follow me."

Is the call enough? Jesus' disciples had the advantage of being with him 24/7. Disciples today do not. They seek to follow someone they've never met. For them, there is only the invitation. It doesn't seem like much to go on.

In some ways, it isn't. In themselves, the words mean nothing, but the person who is calling animates the call. Not just anyone is calling; it's Jesus calling. That makes the question of Jesus' identity more important: Who is this man?

John's gospel addresses this question in a series of stunning responses that are unique to the Gospel. While the logic of discipleship in Matthew's gospel works through blessing, the logic of discipleship in John's gospel works through identification. As he identifies himself, Jesus identifies his disciples: "I AM" becomes "YOU ARE."

࿔

How does this identification happen?

I wrote this book to find out. It does not assume extensive theological knowledge or even a robust background in Sunday school. It does not resort to jargon; it favors anecdote over analysis. More than anything else, I want to see if John's gospel has any traction for the present.

After an initial look at three worlds in play in the interpretation of any piece of literature, the argument treats themes featured in the gospel itself.

- *Collision of Worlds:* Chapter 1 looks at how an ancient text generates insight for contemporary disciples and seekers. Insight happens as a result of the collision of three worlds: the world *behind* the text, the world *of* the text, and the world *in front of* the text. What insights might this collision of worlds in John's gospel generate for disciples today? Subsequent chapters treat five salient features of the Gospel that have traction for disciples today: attention to time, vivid encounters, provocative questions, identity matters, and the presence of the spirit.

- *Attention to Time:* Chapter 2 attends to time by examining beginnings. First words matter in all the Gospels. But the first words of John's gospel remind readers of the first words of the Genesis stories of creation, an intentional echo. Attention to time, particularly to beginnings, keeps disciples on track.

- *Vivid Encounters:* Chapter 3 focuses on the Gospel's encounters between Jesus and characters who are both memorable and fully-developed. More than any other Gospel, John crackles with lively conversation. These encounters continue to direct disciples today.

- *Provocative Questions:* Chapter 4 probes the questions that prompt conversation along the way. In the world according to John, discipleship invites inquiry. Following the questions keeps disciples on track.

- *Identity Matters:* Chapter 5 addresses the central question in John's gospel: "Who are you?" John's Jesus addresses the question of identity in a series of stunning "I AM" sayings and, in doing so, he identifies the people who travel with him.

- *Presence of the Spirit:* Finally, Chapter 6 proposes a series of Spirit-shaped and Spirit-shaping practices that orient disciples along the way. Like bread for the journey, the practices of discernment, friendship, and forgiveness sustain disciples as they follow.

"Are you a practicing Christian?" my friend had asked. I gave her a flippant reply: "No, I got it right the first time."

But in truth, it got me. Like the first followers in the first chapter of John's gospel, I am still simply dazzled by this person called Jesus. And, like the exasperated Thomas, I too explode in frustration: "*Where are we going?*" Discipleship in the key of John has room for intense attraction and equally intense disenchantment.

But underneath surface dazzle and gnawing doubt, I love the way this Gospel treats the Big Questions, the ones that wake me in the middle of the night:

- What time is it? Where did we come from? And where are we going?
- Who's going with me?
- Are these the right questions? What's missing?
- Who are we?
- How can we find our way forward?

In its attention to time, vivid encounters, provocative questions, concern for identity, and orienting practices, John's gospel speaks across the centuries.

Let's listen.

All biblical citations are from the New Revised Standard Version of the Bible, unless otherwise noted.

CHAPTER 1

# Worlds in Collision

TRAVELING TO ISTANBUL DROPPED me into a different world: the smells, the sights, the aesthetic of the city itself. On a busy shopping street, I stopped to admire a display of Turkish carpets. Catching the morning light, the silk fibers in the rugs shone. As I stopped to admire, I caught a glimpse of myself in the shop window, looking.

Travel is a window and a mirror. It opens a window onto other worlds; it holds up a mirror to one's own world. All of these views matter. An attentive traveler registers it all, what she's learned by looking and what she's learned by watching herself look. Travel is both seeing and being seen.[1]

Reading texts, particularly a sacred text like John's gospel, is a lot like travel. It functions as a window onto other worlds and as a mirror to one's own. John's gospel comes out of a distinctive context, opening to its readers windows on other cultures: the world *behind* the text. An expert could "read" the rugs in that shop window in Istanbul, tracing patterns to a particular place. There are worlds behind each Gospel narrative as well. Understanding them illumines the world behind the text.

But the text creates a world of its own: the world *of* the text. Whoever wrote John's gospel edited context, the world behind the text, to make an argument about discipleship. In Istanbul no two shop windows were alike. Each aimed to convince buyers its

---

1. Anthropologist Mary Louise Pratt talks about travel as both "seeing" and "being seen seeing." Pratt, *Imperial Eyes.*

merchandise was the most compelling. In similar fashion, each Gospel makes a distinctive argument about discipleship, organizing the story of Jesus to most effectively make its point. This is the world of the text.

Finally, every text functions as a mirror, challenging readers to acknowledge their own reflections: the world *in front of* the text. It forces readers to reexamine their own expectations. What are they looking for? I stood in front of a shop window, looking at rugs and caught a glimpse of myself looking. When I did, I became keenly aware that these rugs activated an aesthetic imagination I don't use much at home. I resolved to feed that imagination upon returning. By extension, attending to the world in front of the text challenges readers to probe the reflection in the mirror.

Insight occurs when these three worlds collide. The impact creates that "aha!" moment that makes the familiar text suddenly "ring true." Insight sparks when these worlds come into play:

- a truthful rendering of the context in which the text was written: the world *behind* the text;

- a truthful account of the author's intent: the world *of* the text; and

- finally, a truthful awareness of what experience, context, and expectations readers bring to the text: the world *in front of* the text.[2]

If John's gospel makes a particular argument for discipleship, how does that sacred text generate insight for disciples today? Here's a traveler's guide to each world.

## The World Behind The Text: Context

The gospel comes from *somewhere*, a particular time and place. What were the social, political, ethnic, and economic realities peculiar to that time and place? How do they play out in the text? Attending to this world asks that we attend to the context behind

2. Schneiders, *The Revelatory Text.*

a given text. Three dimensions of John's context require attention: an emerging tension between Christians and Jews; the extension of the mission of Christianity to non-Jews; and the delay of the *parousia*, or the return of Jesus to his followers.

## The Jewish Background

Jesus was a Jew.[3] To a greater and lesser degree, all of the Gospels presume their audience would be familiar with Jewish practice and prophecy.

The most important aspect of being Jewish in first-century Palestine was that Jews lived in a land occupied by the Romans. Romans ruled the "chosen people" with an iron hand. While they recognized Judaism as a legitimate religion within the empire (*religio licita*) and allowed Jews their own courts, currency, and religious practices, the Romans taxed the Jews heavily and restricted their mobility.

For Jewish religious leaders, the price of occupation was accommodation. Doubly scrutinized by the Romans and by their own people, these leaders presided over an uneasy peace. Groups known as the "Herodians" or "Sadducees" functioned as ritual leaders. They tended the Temple at Jerusalem, which was destroyed in 70 CE, but was intact at the time of Jesus. Connection to the Temple meant these groups were *place-based.*

"Pharisees" and "scribes" interpreted Torah, applying Jewish law to on-the-ground situations. Unlike the ritual leaders who were tethered to the Temple at Jerusalem, these teachers and lawyers were highly mobile. They went where people needed them, working in the streets and teaching in synagogues scattered across the empire. Connection to the Torah rather than the Temple meant these groups were *text-based,* unbound to place.

When the Romans razed the Temple at Jerusalem in 70 CE, the place-based leadership of Temple priests, the "Herodians," and the "Sadducees," found themselves under threat and out of work.

---

3. Cf. Vermes, *Jesus the Jew* and *The Religion of Jesus the Jew.*

The Pharisees and scribes, on the other hand, packed up their texts and left Jerusalem. They sustained the rituals and practices of the faith in synagogues. Although most of them were written after 70 CE, the stories the Gospels tell about Jesus mentioning all of these leaders.

Ordinary Jews were doubly taxed. They owed taxes both to the Romans and to their own religious leaders. Different currencies were required for each. The Romans required payment in the Roman denarii, which had the Caesar's image on its face, while Jews required payment in shekels, minas, and talents. Converting currencies made money changing a necessary, though despised, occupation. New Testament accounts reveal the strain of this system of double taxation, as well as a general dislike of tax collectors and money changers.

Taxes paid to the religious authorities supported upkeep of the Temple at Jerusalem, the poor, and the religious leaders themselves. Jews who couldn't keep up with their taxes fell into the category of the "unrighteous," while those who could were labeled "righteous." Wealth, rather than good deeds, sharply separated "righteousness" from "unrighteousness."

Occupation by the Romans created among the people a longing for liberation, a time when the chosen land would be returned to the chosen people. They hoped the "messiah" would be a military hero, someone who would rise up out of the desert to rid the promised land of an occupying army. Much of the drama of the Gospels revolves around the dissonance between the longing for a revolutionary hero and Jesus' real identity. John's gospel addresses the dissonance directly. It revolves around a question that comes up early on in the story—"Who are you?"—a question that it answers in a series of "I AM" sayings.

In the absence of liberation, the Jewish people longed for some kind of evidence that God still cared about them. Prophecy counted as a clear sign. At the time of Jesus, the voice of prophecy had been silent in Israel for more than 600 years. When prophets had been around, people did not welcome them. They squirmed under their scolding; they shirked their advice. Now, however, they yearned for an indication of God's continuing solicitude. Because they wanted to believe they still mattered, people mistook Jesus or John the Baptist again and again as a "prophet."

All of the Gospels depict a certain tension between Christians and Jews. A Jewish court, the Sanhedrin, first tried Jesus for religious offenses. Because it could not impose the death penalty, it then turned Jesus over to the Roman courts to be tried for treason. Although each of the Gospels depicts Jesus as emphatically denying any revolutionary intent, the Sanhedrin knew that a political traitor could threaten the fragile equilibrium between the occupiers and the occupied.

The tension between Jews and these earliest followers of Jesus only heightened in the years after Jesus' death. Two events brought the conflict between Jews and Christians out into the open, and both occurred before any of the Gospels were written down.

In July 64 CE, the Emperor Nero (54–68 CE) blamed Christians in Rome for a fire that devastated the city. Accordingly, the emperor rounded up Christian leaders and executed them as punishment. The persecution indicates that the Romans perceived a distinction between Jews and Christians less than a generation after Jesus' death in 30–33 CE. It further reveals that Christians did not qualify at this time as a legitimate religion in the empire (*religio licita*).

A second conflict was an uprising in Jerusalem that began when a priest at the Temple refused to offer prayers for the emperor. The conflict quickly escalated. Rome retaliated with devastating force, destroying the Temple in 70 CE, slaughtering a Jewish army outside of Jerusalem at Masada, and exiling large portions of the population. The Pharisees and scribes moved across the Jordan to Jamnia, and interpretation of Torah replaced worship at the Temple. But the uprising and its aftermath constituted a crisis in Judaism and further separated Christians from Jews.

## Beyond the Jews

Although John's gospel assumes its readers have some knowledge of Judaism, it also signals that this new religion moves beyond it. Jesus' encounters with "outsiders" testify to the author's inclusive intent. Jesus speaks with a Samaritan woman at a time when Samaritans and Jews were bitter enemies. He works with people from his own faith community who would have been labeled "unrighteous." He saves a woman from stoning by inviting anyone without sin to cast the first stone. He risks ritual impurity by raising a man from the dead. In the presence of religious leaders who are eager to equate infirmity with sin, Jesus heals a man blind from birth. Encounters with those who are decidedly "unrighteous" or outside the house of Israel telegraph the Gospel's reach to John's audience and to our own. Jesus came to the "lost sheep of the house of Israel," but also to "lost sheep" everywhere.

## Delay of the Parousia

Jesus promised to return, known in Greek as the *parousia*. But he didn't come back when people thought he would. Earliest Christians expected his imminent return. As the original disciples died or were executed, the communities they left behind hunkered down for the long haul.[4] These communities organized their common life, set up standards for leadership, and established governing documents. They formalized rituals for initiation and for sharing the sacred meal. Most importantly, they began to write things down. Though these documents present themselves as authentic writings from the original disciples, it was the deaths of the original disciples that prompted them. The four Gospels come from a second generation of believers who dedicated themselves to preserving the memory, the teachings, and the story of Jesus.

Probably the first written accounts of Jesus' story were narratives of the passion and resurrection, followed by a series of sayings attributed to him. Undoubtedly, these accounts were organized to

4. Cf., Brown, *The Churches the Apostles Left Behind*.

address the pastoral needs of particular communities. Luke's gospel alludes to a proliferation of "Gospels." "Many have undertaken to set down an orderly account of the events that have been fulfilled among us . . ." (Luke 1:1).

Four accounts passed into the tradition as authoritative.

Written soon after the destruction of the Temple at Jerusalem in 70 CE, Mark is the evangelist in a hurry.[5] Wasting no time with birth narratives, the story begins with the adult Jesus' baptism and rushes into his ministry. The narrative hurtles toward the crucifixion and the empty tomb.

Matthew's gospel introduces Jesus not simply as a rabbi or teacher, but as the embodiment of a new law. Significantly, disciples follow a person, more complex than merely following the rules. Written around 80 CE, the text assumes familiarity with Judaism but reaches beyond the "chosen people" to include outsiders.

Written around 90–110 CE, Luke's gospel originally included what is now Acts. Together they comprise the "acts of the Spirit," and the whole plays as one of the most lyrical accounts of Jesus' life, death, and resurrection, one full of songs and a passion for the poor.

Finally, there is John's gospel, which would be hard to use for a Christmas pageant, as it offers no manger and no fluffy sheep with shepherds tending their flocks by night. The birth of discipleship matters to this author. Indeed, the Gospel claims to be the account of a disciple, "the disciple whom Jesus loves" (John 13:23). What's the point this Gospel wants to make?

## The World of the Text: The Gospel Itself

Regardless of the world that generates it, the text creates a world of its own. The author of John's gospel advances an argument about discipleship. He constructs a particular portrait of Jesus, which

---

5. Mark was written shortly after the destruction of the Temple at Jerusalem in 70 CE. Known as the "little apocalypse," Mark 13 foreshadows the carnage of the destruction of the Temple, seeming to prophesy something that for the author's actual audience had already happened.

then defines those who follow him. In John's gospel, Jesus expresses God's love for the world. Accordingly, love sums up John's distinctive version of discipleship in "the beloved community." The question for Christians, then and now, remains: How do disciples love in the way we have been loved?

Writing as the "beloved" disciple, the author assures the audience that his "testimony is true" (John 21:24). That testimony falls into two major parts: a book of "signs and wonders" (John 1:19–12:50) and a lengthy farewell discourse (John 13–17).[6]

The first part argues God loved the world enough to enter it as a human being (John 3:16). As proof of that argument, the narrative then describes "signs and wonders" that this God-human does to address the state of the world: miracles like turning water into wine, healings like restoring sight to a man blind from birth, even a resurrection.

The second part of the Gospel gives Jesus' "farewell discourse (John 13–17) and describes a Last Supper that features not food but feet. If the first part of John's gospel reveals Jesus to be God in human form, the second part of John's Gospel tells disciples how to behave as followers of such a God: ". . . love one another as I have loved you" (John 15:12).

The entire Gospel leads to this final counsel. This is the world of the text, the canvas on which the author paints his striking portrait of Jesus. Five distinctive features stand out: attention to time, vivid encounters, provocative questions, identity issues, and the presence of the Spirit.

## Attention to Time

Mark may be the evangelist in a hurry, but John is the one who watches the clock. An awareness of time pulses through the Gospel. The author registers the Jewish liturgical year, its festivals, and

---

6. The first major part of the Gospel, the book of "signs and wonders," is preceded by a prologue, John 1:1–18. The second major part of the Gospel, the "farewell discourse," is followed by passion and resurrection stories (John 18-20) and an epilogue (John 21).

its Sabbaths, and he coordinates Jesus' ministry with that calendar. He pegs key events to certain hours of the day and days of the week; he attends to the sun's movements, marking daybreak, midday, and evening. Why the concern for time? Certainly, there may be a deliberate attempt to pattern Jesus' ministry along the lines of a new creation, as I argue in the next chapter. Further, given all the accounts of the life of Jesus that must have been around by the time this latest of the Gospels appeared, its author wants to establish a credible, even authoritative sequence of events for his own history.

There may be a pedagogical thrust to the author's attention to time as well. These careful calibrations of clock and calendar point to the only sense of time that matters: God's time. It's a time zone unknown to Greenwich Mean. Responding at one point to the disciples' request to be more public about who he is, Jesus counters: "My time has not yet come, *but your time is always here*" (John 7:6). The question turns back onto the disciples. What time is it? How will they number their days?

## Vivid Encounters

Perhaps the three most important words in the Judaeo-Christian sacred texts are the words: "But God said . . . ." Narration handles the relatively unimportant material: "They went here and did this and talked about the weather." Direct speech delivers the important material.

John's gospel features a lot of direct speech, much of it from Jesus. Every "sign" and "wonder" comes with a lengthy explanation. Jesus engages a Samaritan woman in a long conversation, unusual because she's both a female and a foreigner to him. The healing of a lame man instigates another long explanation to the Jewish authorities. The feeding of the 5,000 launches an extended discourse on food. In John's gospel, every miracle or healing comes with an explanation, leaving readers or hearers to wonder if the disciples might have needed one.

Conversation provokes encounter, particularly the edgy, authentic conversations that Jesus has. In the process, the characters of all parties emerge. John's gospel offers carefully wrought portraits of people whom the other Gospels present as mere props. The gospel is crowded, populated by vivid characters who have minds of their own—and who speak them. Conversation fills out the contours of character, and both parties become more defined.

## Provocative Questions

Questions dominate the encounters in John's gospel. In fact, a powerful question, directed to John the Baptist, launches the Gospel itself: "Who are you?" (John 1:19)

Who is John the Baptist? Who is Jesus? Who are the people who follow him? The questions orient the Gospel: they set the tone in style and in content. John's Jesus leads by inquiry. Indeed, the first words out of Jesus' mouth are a question: "What are you looking for?" (John 1:38). With this question Jesus probes disciples' deepest longing, because he knows they'll all be projected onto him, preventing people from seeing who he really is.

The questions of John's gospel come in many and various ways. Often, Jesus responds to a question with only another question. The author of John's gospel builds his argument for discipleship by asking questions and noting questions posed by Jesus and questions posed to him. The questions, their kind and range, bear greater scrutiny, but clearly John's Jesus is a Socratic Jesus, a teacher who instructs by asking questions.[7]

## Identity Matters

The question of identity animates the entire Gospel, from the initial encounter with John to a final encounter with the risen Christ on the shores of the Sea of Tiberias. From start to finish, no one sees who Jesus really is, and he becomes a blank screen for all of

7. Cf. Dear, *The Questions of Jesus*.

their projections: Elijah, the prophet, a king, a revolutionary, even a gardener. The author, through Jesus' own utterances, aims to clear up the confusion, and he does so in a series of "I AM" sayings that are distinctive to this Gospel.

Questions of identity hound Jesus' followers as well. Then as now, people were known by the company they kept. After Jesus' arrest, servants catch Peter lingering nearby. They ask him a variation of the Gospel's signature question: "Who are you?" Strikingly, they pose the question in the negative: "You are not also one of this man's disciples, are you?" (John 18:17). In denying whom he follows, Peter denies himself. Who is Peter, really? And who are the people who follow Jesus, then and now? Who Jesus is defines people who follow him.

## The Presence of the Spirit

Finally, John's gospel pays a great deal of attention to spirits, situating the Gospel firmly in the context of Jewish longing for the return of the spirit of prophecy in their midst.

John's audience believed in spirits. They inhabited people, places, and things, working for good or ill. Spirit possession could go either way. People like Jesus and John the Baptist possessed spirits of powerful goodness, while others were possessed of "demons" or "evil spirits."

John's gospel pays particular attention to the spirit of the risen Christ and how it can be discerned amidst all the other spirits of the age. John's Jesus promises disciples that he will send his spirit to guide them. The question for them is whether they will recognize Jesus' spirit in the midst of all the others. All of the "I AM" sayings function against the horizon of this promise. They not only tell disciples who Jesus is, they help them recognize a spirit of Jesus that is still in the world. Much of the Gospel works to help people distinguish this spirit from all the others.

## The World In Front Of The Text

Finally, John's gospel is more than a text: it is a *sacred* text. That means it speaks with authority to the community of people who continue to call themselves disciples today. They call it "Scripture," and they do so because they believe it has something to say to them now, both as communities and as individuals. It speaks as a living word into the present moment. Biblical archeologists describe the world *behind* the text. Literary critics reconstitute the world *of* the text; communities of disciples try to discern its meaning for the present. The dialogue with the world in front of the text again touches on key themes of John's gospel—attention to time, vivid encounters, provocative questions, identity matters, and the presence of the spirit.

## Attention to Time

As a seminar began, the speaker walked to the podium, looked confused, and asked: "What time is it?" We reached for our smart phones and checked our watches. "No," she said. "I mean, what *time* is it?" She kept pressing the question, over and over again, as we identified the kinds of time we keep: by calendar, by clock, by season, by the moon, by the academic year, and on and on and on.

Chronological time marches forward in linear fashion, and there's no repeating it. Right now it is 8:08 AM on a Wednesday morning in July, 2015. It will never be this time again. No can someone scroll back to being twenty-four years old again, even if he wanted to.

Other time moves in circles. The earth spins in its daily round. The moon rotates around the earth. Seasons make an annual circuit. Day fades into to darkness, which opens to a new day.

Because historically liturgical time synched with annual, seasonal, and diurnal movements, it moves in circles. Sabbath ends every week for Jews, where Sunday begins the week for Christians. Rosh Hashanah begins the new year for Jews; Advent, for Christians. Islam follows a lunar calendar. In so many of the world's religions, liturgical time is cyclical.

For all its attention to chronological time, John's gospel worries about a different kind of time entirely: God's time. Telling God's time requires a discernment that doesn't depend on a watch. Exceeding both linear and cyclical time, God's time is *kairotic* time. Kairotic time is chronological time that gets absorbed by the mystery it bears. Sometimes religious ritual trespasses into God's time; sometimes beauty cracks through. When it does, disciples know they're in a different time zone entirely. John's gospel urges them to pay attention to time, particularly to the time of beginnings.

## Vivid Encounters

Technology makes it possible to encounter people face-to-screen instead of face-to-face. It enables conversation in text and sound bite. Emoticons communicate feeling. There's time to respond—or not; there's time to consider—or shoot off a rapid-fire rejoinder.

Even on a superficial level, John's gospel confronts the world in front of this text with people who cannot be selected from a contact list and situations that cannot be controlled. Moreover, people seem to speak their minds freely and without fear. Finally, in John's gospel Jesus runs into people a good Jew would not have chosen to hang out with. They are outside his class, beyond his comfort zone, and off limits to religious protocol.

Jesus' encounters with the socially and culturally marginalized of his time invite readers and hearers of this Gospel to consider the divisions in their own culture: people of another race or gender or sexual orientation, immigrants or residents, progressives or conservatives, Christians or non-Christians, fundamentalists of left, right, and center. Jesus' encounters prompt reconsideration of whoever qualifies as "outcast" or "enemy" today.

Reconsidering the whole category of "enemy," both having one and being one, John's gospel points in the direction of love. Returning as the risen Christ to friends who'd betrayed him, Jesus could have treated the disciples as "enemies." Instead, he brought his friends peace. He challenges twenty-first-century disciples to do the same.

## Provocative Questions

"What should I do?" a student asked, trying to work through a conflict between work and family. We wrestled with her question, until I posed a different one: "Where's the invitation in all of this?" Slowly the ground shifted; she had a new angle of vision. Questions demand answers, but sometimes it's worth pausing to see if the question being addressed is the right one.

Because John's Socratic Jesus asks and is asked so many questions, the Gospel invites consideration of the questions themselves. Sometimes asking a different question reframes a difficult situation. Sometimes a question has no immediate answer. The point is to simply "live the questions."[8] Paying attention to the questions of John's gospel invites us to attend to the questions in our own lives and in our own times.

## Identity Matters

"Who are you?" When asked, a woman gave her full birth name, impressive in length, then smiled and said, "But just call me Becky." An older man answered with his place of birth: "I'm a Montanan." A twenty-something first gave his profession: an engineer. Another woman identified by political affiliation: "I'm an Independent." An Indian scientist eagerly laid out a family tree. Who are you? A key question in John's gospel provokes lots of answers.

Who are you? Historian of American religion Diana Butler Bass asks a different question: "*Whose* are you?" Belonging determines identity—and in crucial ways. Where prior generations of Americans defined themselves by believing or behaving, what they believed in or how they conducted their lives, people

---

8. Rilke, *Letters to a Young Poet*. Also available at http://carrothers.com/rilke4.htm.

in twenty-first-century America identify by affiliation: belonging. Whose are you?[9] John's gospel raises the question: Whose are we? What's our primary identity, that identity for which we might have to put our lives on the line?[10]

## The Presence of Spirit

Large numbers of Americans regard themselves as "nones."[11] They declare their dependence from organized religions entirely, maintaining they are "spiritual but not religious."

John's gospel remains convinced that there are a lot of spirits out there, some of them not so benign. The ancient world had fairly vigorous practices for discerning the spirits. John's practice of discernment boils it all down to love: "Love one another as I have loved you" (John 15:12). This Gospel presents a more difficult challenge: How would Jesus love? Living into this question means regarding the other and naming the other not as enemy or stranger but as friend. Calling disciples "friends" rather than servants, Jesus offers friendship as the form of that love. When he returns after the resurrection, Jesus forgives the friends who had betrayed him. Moreover, he charges them with a ministry of reconciliation. Forgiveness animates the love to which disciples witness in the world. In living the question itself—"How would Jesus love?"—disciples discover the directions to the Spirit of the risen Christ in the world today.

9. Bass, *Christianity After Religion*.

10. Hear the taxonomy of belonging from Paul's letter to the Corinthians: "You belong to Christ, and Christ belongs to God" (1 Cor 3:23).

11. "Nones" are people who claim no religious affiliation. When presented with an option to self-identify as Protestant, Catholic, Jew, Muslim, Mormon, etc., they check the box next to "none." Sometimes these people identify as "spiritual but not religious"; sometimes they call themselves atheist or agnostic. For more information, see the ongoing "Religious Landscape Study": http://www.pewforum.org/religious-landscape-study/.

See also David Crumm, "Are Americans Becoming Less Religious?" in *Trust*, February 4, 2016. http://magazine.pewtrusts.org/en/archive/winter-2016/are-americans-becoming-less-religious.

Reading John's gospel through the lens of the world in front of the text reveals aspects of that world that disciples might otherwise miss. Attention to the world in front of the text requires careful attention to today's contexts and communities.

Insight sparks at the intersection of three worlds, the world behind the text, the world of the text, and the world in front of the text. When these three worlds come together, a text suddenly "rings true," particularly for disciples wondering how to respond to Jesus' call today.

CHAPTER 2

# Attention to Time: First Words

RACING THROUGH AN AIRPORT, late for a flight, I overheard a shred of conversation: "And the first words out of her mouth were—" the rest of the conversation was lost. As I buckled into my seat, I thought about how much people pay attention to first words. They create lasting impressions; they unlock character. First words send a message, and each Gospel sends a different one. Before examining the first words of John's gospel and the first words of its key character, Jesus, it is worth understanding its distinctiveness in comparison to the other Gospels.

## First Words In The Four Gospels

Mark's gospel, the earliest account to be written down, opens with the intention to tell "the beginning of the good news of Jesus Christ, the Son of God" (Mark 1:1). The author identifies Jesus at the outset as the "Son of God," but it's an identity the disciples never quite grasp. Despite the fact they are with Jesus 24/7, they remain clueless about who he really is. Instead, they project onto Jesus their own deep needs for a military leader, a rabbi, and a prophet. Only outsiders, the demons, and a Roman centurion at the crucifixion scene recognize Jesus as "the Son of God."[1]

1. Cf. Mark 1:24; 5:7; 15:39.

The Gospel of Matthew begins with "Jesus the Messiah, the son of David, the son of Abraham" (Matt 1:1), presenting a full genealogy as proof. But as careful readers trace the bloodlines, they find a lineage that leads to Joseph, not Jesus, and the story emphasizes that Joseph is not Jesus' father. Moreover the genealogy itself, which begins by moving from father to son, or patrilineally, interjects the names of women who are not necessarily of the Hebrew people but nonetheless prove key to their survival:

- Tamar: When she was widowed and left childless by her Hebrew husband, Tamar was denied justice by his family. Religious law required her dead husband's brother to impregnate her so that she would have a child who could care for her. Widows without children faced an uncertain future. Her brother-in-law Onan slept with her, but withdrew before ejaculating, spilling his seed on the ground. Denied an heir, Tamar took matters into her own hands. Disguised as a prostitute, she seduced her father-in-law Judah in order to become pregnant and secure an heir. Tamar, her twin sons Perez and Zerah, and their father (and her father-in-law!) make it into the genealogy (Gen 38).

- Rahab: The book of Joshua identifies Rahab as a "prostitute" and a Canaanite woman who secured Joshua's safe passage into the land of Canaan (Josh 2:1–7).

- Ruth: A Moabite woman widowed by a Hebrew man, Ruth remained faithful to her embittered, bereaved Hebrew mother-in-law Naomi/Mara, returning with her to Bethlehem, marrying a Hebrew man, and bearing children that would ensure their well-being (Ruth).

- Bathsheba: "The wife of Uriah the Hittite," Bathsheba was raped and made pregnant by King David, who then arranged for her Hittite husband to be killed in battle (2 Sam 11).

- Mary: The mother of Jesus was a woman pregnant outside of marriage, a situation punishable by death.

Powerful women interrupt the bloodline from father to son. More importantly, the stories of these women speak of a need for justice, safety, and restitution, needs that have not diminished today. Different branches have been grafted onto this family tree, and the line from Joseph and Mary forward promises to be equally diverse. Only after this powerfully inclusive genealogy does Matthew's gospel proceed with a birth narrative.

Luke's gospel promises "an orderly account" (Luke 1:1), beginning with the birth of John the Baptist. But the Gospel gets sidetracked by a soundtrack, featuring the lyrics of two canticles (the *Magnificat*, Mary's song, and the *Benedictus*, or the Song of Zechariah) before even getting to the story of Jesus' birth.

Mary packs all the hopes for her newborn into a song that reads like a political manifesto, identifying the reversals Jesus' birth inaugurates. The mighty will be laid low and the lowly, exalted; the hungry will be fed, and the rich "will be sent away empty" (Luke 1:48–55). Then the mute priest and elderly father of John the Baptist, Zechariah, breaks his silence with a song announcing the birth of a child who will "prepare the way" for Mary's son (Luke 1:68–79). The story of Jesus' birth only happens after all the singing stops.

First words send a message, and John's gospel sends several, both in the way the Gospel itself begins and in the first words the Gospel ascribes to Jesus.

It's important to notice how the story *doesn't* begin. The fourth gospel offers up no story of Jesus' birth. Absent are the angels, the magi, the shepherds, and the sheep. There is no angelic appearance to a virgin announcing her pregnancy. There is not even a baby Jesus. In fact, when Jesus first appears in the Gospel, he's an adult, walking, talking, and full of questions. Anyone planning a Sunday school Christmas pageant based on the Gospel according to John might as well give up and go home. There are no parts for the children to play. John's gospel seems targeted to grown-ups.

The Gospel begins with another birth narrative.

> In the beginning was the Word,
> and the Word was with God,

and the Word was God.

He was in the beginning with God.

All things came into being through him,

and without him not one thing came into being (John 1:1–4).

John's story opens with the birth of everything. Here "the Word" gives birth to the entire creation. Recalling the creation narratives in the book of Genesis, this Gospel's first birth narrative is *cosmic*. When Jesus walks into the story as an adult, the story turns to a second birth narrative, the birth of discipleship. This narrative is *communal*. He calls Andrew, Simon Peter, and Nathanael, and as a distinctive group forms around him the characters of each emerge in sharp detail.

Creation and community: These narratives build an arc of discipleship in the Gospel, an account that is literally "time sensitive."

## First Words In John's Gospel

### The Birth of the Cosmos: Creation

A few years ago a friend invited me to climb Mount Kilimanjaro. Kilimanjaro hadn't been on my bucket list. It was a time in my life when bucket lists seemed like a luxury that had simply passed me by. I had lost my husband to brain cancer the year before, and the lists that ran our lives were lists of treatments, surgeries, and doctors' appointments. Then one day all that ended. The only lists I had numbered the organizations that needed death certificates. I was broken, in pieces, and quite literally list-less. When I received an invitation to climb Kilimanjaro, I shrugged—listlessly—and said: "Sure. Why not?"

One morning a few months later, I found myself at the base of the mountain. We climbed through the rain forest, steamy and close with the calls of strange birds. There was evening and there was morning, a second day.

We climbed through the alpine meadow, filled with scrub trees green against red volcanic rock. There was evening and there was morning, a third day.

We climbed above the tree line, into a zone where plants hugged the ground, bursting with color from every crevasse and cranny, and we learned the hearty species that survive altitude and intense swings in temperature. The air thinned; oxygen grew more precious. We found a rhythm of walking that allowed for steady forward motion, no matter how slow, so that we weren't stopping and starting all the time. We found a rhythm of breathing that allowed for steady respiration, no matter how shallow, so that we weren't gasping for air. There was evening and there was morning, a fourth day.

We climbed out of the realm of vegetation entirely, entering the fierce landscape of the summit itself. Here there was nothing but scree, searing sun, and shards of volcanic rock. It looked like we'd stumbled into a giants' kitchen in which there had been a domestic argument the night before. The volcanic blast littered the ground with fragments that looked like pieces of red-clay pottery. Here was a once-perfect bowl, angrily smashed into pieces; there, a plate, shattered beyond repair; up ahead, a cup, dashed into fragments. There was evening and—

At midnight we made the final ascent to the summit. By that time, like the landscape around us, we ourselves were in pieces, shattered by exhaustion, thin air, and the cold. The only thing that kept me going was the pull of the hundreds of climbers in front of us, the push of hundreds from behind. Broken as we were by altitude and exertion, together we snaked up the mountain like something alive, our headlamps pricks of light in an inky darkness. There was the rest of that night and there was morning, a fifth day.

As that morning dawned, we stood at the summit and surveyed the wreckage we'd spent the night climbing through. As I looked at the earth's curvature gently falling around us, I remember thinking: This whole mountain is one huge mound of broken pieces. Yet, there it was, Africa's "Shining Mountain," the highest peak on the continent. Out of these pieces, a new creation.

These images stuck with me, like scraps of an insistent rhyme that I could neither shake nor completely make out. Then, I started to hear it everywhere: the refrain of breaking and remaking, breaking and remaking. Out of these pieces, a new creation. The refrain plays out in both Genesis and the Gospel of John.

Breaking and remaking: It's the story of the Genesis account of creation. For life to emerge, that smooth stone of matter, "without form and void," had to be shattered. The cosmos emerges out of distinction and division, separation and breakage. Listen to the pattern:

> Let there be a dome in the midst of the waters,
> and let it separate the waters from the waters (Gen 1:6).

> Let the waters under the sky be gathered together in one place,
> and let dry land appear (Gen 1:9).

> Let there be lights in the dome of the sky to separate the day
> from the night (Gen 1:14).

Light is broken away from darkness, day from night, the heavens from the earth, the sun from the moon and all stars. Out of these pieces, a new creation.

Nor are humans spared the breakage. In a second story of creation, God breaks open Adam to create a partner, removing part of his rib to fashion Eve. Adam himself appears to have been wrested from the earth, torn out of an environment he was part of. Poet and painter William Blake (1757–1827) captures the moment in a watercolor that shows God literally pulling Adam from an earth that wants to keep him. As Blake paints it, a snake wraps around Adam's leg, pulling him into the earth. God reaches for a rock with his left hand and lifts Adam's head with his right. Both faces are anguished, and the painting telegraphs energy, even trauma.[2] New beginnings emerge from the broken pieces of something else. Yet, out of these pieces, a new creation.

---

2. William Blake, "Elohim Creating Adam," *Large Colour Prints*, 1795, Tate Gallery: London. Blake believed the painting captured the moment

Breaking and remaking: It's John's story of creation as well. The Gospel invokes the Genesis creation stories in an opening hymn.

> In the beginning was the Word, and the Word was with God, and the Word was God. He was in the beginning with God. All things came into being through him, and without him not one thing came into being. What has come into being in him was life, and the life was the light of all people. The light shines in the darkness, and the darkness did not overcome it.
>
> There was a man sent from God, whose name was John. He came as a witness to testify to the light, so that all might believe through him. He himself was not the light, but he came to testify to the light. The true light, which enlightens everyone, was coming into the world.
>
> He was in the world, and the world came into being through him; yet the world did not know him. He came to what was his own, and his own people did not accept him. But to all who received him, who believed in his name, he gave power to become children of God, who were born, not of blood or of the will of the flesh or of the will of man, but of God.
>
> And the Word became flesh and lived among us, and we have seen his glory, the glory as of a father's only son, full of grace and truth. (John testified to him and cried out, 'This was he of whom I said, "He who comes after me ranks ahead of me because he was before me."') From his fullness we have all received, grace upon grace. The law indeed was given through Moses; grace and truth came through Jesus Christ. No one has ever seen God. It is God the only Son, who is close to the Father's heart, who has made him known (John 1:1–18).

Any Jew hearing these words would have recognized in them the cadence of Genesis. Different in tone and style from the rest of

---

of the "fall," which for him was not a matter of disobeying a command but receiving a material body. If so, the illustration depicts a double breakage. Adam's spirit is broken out of the spiritual realm; Adam's body is broken apart from the earth. Available at http://www.tate.org.uk/art/artworks/blake-elohim-creating-adam-n05055.

the Gospel, the hymn is probably an addition to it. Yet, this story of a new creation sets the stage for what follows. Like the Genesis creation stories, themes of light and darkness dominate in John's gospel. Jesus identifies himself as "light," indeed, the "light of the world" (John 8:12). He heals a man born blind (John 9:1–41), prompting Pharisees to wonder about their own capacity for sight. Jesus repeats that he comes as "light," so that people might not "remain in darkness" (John 12:46). In a world without streetlamps and fluorescent lighting, sundown meant darkness. To *have* light signaled wealth; to *be* light signaled supernatural power.

More important, like the Genesis stories, there is breakage. "The true light" breaks away from God to enter a world that "did not know him" and "did not accept him" (John 1:10–11). The Word's journey in John deliberately recalls the breaking and re-making of the Genesis creation stories. And out of these pieces, a new creation.

## The Birth of Discipleship: Community

As the Gospel continues, the creation of the cosmos gives way to the creation of discipleship. A second birth narrative follows the first, one that distinguishes Jesus from John by separating the "light" from the "witness to the light." It opens with followers of John the Baptist breaking away from their old master to follow a new one. The breakage continues.

Approaching the Baptist, Jewish leaders pose to him the central question of the Gospel: "Who are you?" Where the other Gospels embed this question into the middle of Jesus' ministry, John's raises it at the outset. Where the other Gospels put the question in Jesus' mouth, John's gospel hands it off to the leaders of the people: "Who are you?" Yet across the Gospels, the answers to this pivotal question reflect people's deepest longings:

- they yearn for a Messiah, a revolutionary leader who would defeat the despised Roman army of occupation;

- they yearn for another Elijah, whom legend prophesied would appear just before the day of liberation;

- they yearn for the words of any "prophet," for this would mean the return of prophecy to Israel and presage the day of liberation.

John the Baptist dispenses with all of these expectations in the words of another prophet: "I am the voice of one crying out in the wilderness . . ." (Isa 40:3). When the Baptist hails Jesus as "the lamb of God," two of his disciples break from him immediately to follow this new teacher. Eventually, the confusion between Jesus and John comes to a head, and the two sets of disciples confront one another. As he had done with the Jewish leaders, John the Baptist now denies to his own disciples that he is the "Messiah." He breaks definitively with their projections.

More breakage occurs as Jesus encounters the other disciples. One by one they break from whatever they've been doing—teaching, fishing, collecting taxes, and whomever they've been following—to join up with Jesus.

Later in the story, the cost of discipleship becomes clear. Nothing is going the way the disciples expect, and they murmur against Jesus and one another. He asks if they now want to leave him too. Peter replies: "Lord, to whom shall we go?" (John 6:68). The disciples have permanently broken away from their old lives. Yet, out of these pieces, comes the creation of a community of disciples. John's story of the birth of discipleship parallels the Genesis creation stories in its theme of breaking and remaking.

John's creation story parallels the Genesis accounts in yet another way: its day-by-day chronicling of the birth of discipleship. There's an attention to the seven days of creation in John's opening account of Jesus' ministry, and it must have been deliberate. The leaders of the people interrogate John the Baptist, asking who he really is (John 1:19–28). There is evening and there is morning, a first day. "Then, the next day" (John 1:29), John baptizes Jesus. There is evening and there is morning, a second day.

"The next day" (John 1:35), John stands with two of his disciples and greets Jesus as "the Lamb of God." One of the disciples, Andrew, goes to get his brother, Simon Peter, and the three of them remain with Jesus. There is evening and there is morning, a third day.

"The next day" (John 1:43) Jesus encounters Philip and Nathanael, and they join a growing band of disciples. There is evening and there is morning, a fourth day.

There must have been a fifth day and a sixth day, because "on the third day" after Jesus met Philip and Nathanael, there is a wedding at Cana to which Jesus and his disciples are invited (John 2:1). This would have been on a seventh day. John's creation story concludes a week of new beginnings with a miracle: changing water into wine. "Jesus did this, the first of his signs, in Cana of Galilee, and revealed his glory; and his disciples believed in him" (John 2:11).

The act of belief settles like a blessing on the whole week, echoing the benediction that ends each day of creation in Genesis, as God saw that it was "good." Finally, just as God rested on the seventh day, so all the guests at Cana go down to Capernaum to rest.

John's account recalls the Genesis accounts of creation. Both stories narrate a momentous week. The first week of Jesus' ministry follows the first week of creation, a symmetry that would not have been lost on a Jew.

## First Words Of Jesus

Breaking and remaking, light and darkness, seven days: John's gospel begins with the birth narratives of a new creation and a new community. It's a distinctive message. But how is the main character introduced? What does he say?

The first reported words out of Jesus' mouth set a pattern for who he is and how the author intends to portray him. Three statements in particular are foundational for John's argument about discipleship: "What are you looking for?" "Come and see." "Follow me."

## *"What are you looking for?" (John 1:37)*

Jesus asks this of two disciples of John the Baptist, who then proceed to leave one teacher to follow a new one. Some translations render the Greek as "What do you seek?" or more simply, "What do you want?" Whichever the preferred translation, it's significant that Jesus' first words in John's gospel are a question. The question registers differently depending on emphasis.

***What*** **are you looking for?** Do people always know? The disciples to whom Jesus addressed the question didn't. They thought they were looking for someone like John the Baptist, but when Jesus came along, identified by John as "the Lamb of God," they deserted John to follow Jesus. The quick turnaround suggests they didn't really know what they were looking for at all. It also signals the level of commitment Jesus can expect from such a feckless crew.

Then again, do we always know what we're looking for? In the weeks after my husband died, I spent hours each day losing and finding things. I'd lose an important piece of paper I'd had my hands on the day before. It would be gone, completely vanished. So I'd start looking, trying to reconstruct where I'd been when I last laid hands on the missing object. I'd get more and more frantic until finally I had to sit down and ask myself: "*What* are you looking for?" It became clear to me that I was really looking for *someone* and not *something* at all. That someone wasn't coming back, so I wasn't going to find him. Nothing else really mattered. Facing the hard truth calmed me somehow and invariably allowed me to find what I'd lost. By then the missing object had assumed its proper importance.[3]

---

3. Cf. Joan Didion's memoir of the first year following the death of her husband John Gregory Dunne. Didion, *The Year of Magical Thinking.*

**"What are *you* looking for?"** probes an individual's or a community's deepest desire. Desire is generated internally, while outcomes or expectations are often externally imposed. Discerning desire invites internal probing: what do *you* really seek? Addressing the question takes both insight and wisdom. Insight separates external expectations from internal yearnings; wisdom distinguishes among competing goods. Ignatius Loyola, founder of the Jesuits, or the Society of Jesus, knew the power of desire. He didn't try to subdue or "master" it—because he believed that God worked through desire, not in spite of it. Ignatius developed a set of spiritual exercises designed to *tutor* desires.[4] Discipleship in John's gospel addresses the heart's deepest longings.

**"What are you *looking* for?"** In my own lost-and-found story, the real problem was not what I'd couldn't *find*, but what I couldn't *see*. Grief blinded me, and I couldn't *see* something that was right in front of me. My physical sight was disrupted. Worse, on a deeper level, I couldn't *see* what really mattered. My sense of proportion was skewed, and part of my frustration was not "seeing" what really mattered and what didn't.

Jesus' first words signal the Gospel's concern with seeing things as they really are. The Gospel works on its readers like a series of eye exercises, training them to better see Jesus. At the end of John's gospel, Mary Magdalene looks so hard for the earthly Jesus, she can't *see* the risen Christ right next to her. She mistakes him for a gardener (John 20:15). Jesus corrects the vision of people blinded by loss and poverty, power and ambition, and he does this by revealing to them their deepest needs and then meeting them. The Gospel is not about losing and finding, but looking and actually *seeing*. In the horizon of the author's attention to vision, Jesus' next words make a different kind of sense.

---

4. Cf. Ganss, *Ignatius of Loyola*. An older translation of *The Spiritual Exercises* by Father Elder Mullan, SJ, is available online: http://www.jesuit.org/jesuits/wp-content/uploads/the-spiritual-exercises-.pdf. Accessed July 13, 2015.

*"Come and see" (John 1:39).*

John's disciples respond to Jesus' first words with a question of their own: "Where are you staying?" or "Where do you dwell?" The Greek word for "staying" (*meno,* literally, "to stay" or "to abide" or "to persevere") carries a number of connotations, ranging from physical location to spiritual dwelling place. Most likely, the disciples expect an answer that gives them a street address: "with the family of Simon Peter" or "in the house by the river" or "at the Best Western near the airport." Disciples looking for location want maps, directions, and estimated time of travel. They want to know *where* they can find Jesus. But Jesus doesn't respond with a location.

Maybe the disciples expect Jesus to give his family credentials: "I'm son of Joseph the carpenter from Nazareth, son of Jacob." These disciples want to know status. They need to know *who's* got this man's back, *who* his family is, and whether that crowd can be trusted. But Jesus doesn't respond with a genealogy or a list of references.

Maybe the disciples expect Jesus to produce spiritual credentials: "I am the fulfillment of the messianic prophecy." Disciples looking for spiritual clout want to know Jesus' authority. They want to know *why* they should drop everything and follow this man. Who is *he* following, who's *his* mentor, who's *his* guru? But Jesus doesn't respond by identifying himself as "the Word who was from the beginning with God."

Any of these responses would all be direct answers to the disciples' question. Jesus neither clarifies the question nor does he answer directly. He responds obliquely: "Come and see." The words hold invitation, not direction. They also do not give the disciples actual information. What they find depends on what they seek in the first place, what they *look* for. Finally, what they find in Jesus depends on how good their vision is. Spare, arch, and pointed, the exchange gives away nothing, reveals little, and extends only an offer of relationship. Invitation was enough: "They came and saw where he was staying, and they remained with him that day" (John 1:39).

### *"Follow me." (John 1:43)*

Throughout the gospels, Jesus calls disciples with the words, "Follow me." The only thing he says more often is the caution to "Fear not" or "Be not anxious." That's not a coincidence. Then and now, the journey of discipleship is scary, difficult business.

In John's gospel, the invitation to "Follow me" is distinctive. The words open and close the Gospel. In the beginning of the Gospel, Jesus speaks them to Philip. At the Gospel's conclusion, he speaks them to Peter. John's gospel alone acknowledges that discipleship is such scary, difficult business that disciples will need to hear that invitation to follow again and again to stay on track. The Gospel reassures disciples that Jesus continues to speak those words, if they can but listen.

"Follow me." Only John's Jesus claims: "I AM the way." If disciples want to get where they need to go, they follow a *person* — and not just any person, *this* person. How does that happen?

The most important way to follow this person is to keep him always in front. I remember watching a herd of elephants cross a wadi in central Tanzania. Our group had seen predators in the area, so we were concerned about the elephants' safety, particularly for the calf in their midst. But the guide pointed out the alignment of the herd. The young elephant was surrounded by the herd and directly behind one in particular. It didn't know where it was going. All it could see was that big butt in front of it. But following that offered protection. As long as it knew whom to follow, the calf could cross the wadi in safety.

Followers need to keep track of the person they're following. This obvious insight often eluded the disciples. Like disciples today, they got distracted, bored, or discouraged. When Jesus tells the feckless Peter to "Get behind me" (Mark 8:33), he's only reminding him: "Follow me." Invitation takes the shape of sharp rebuke. Peter needed it. He wanted to take the lead.

Another way to follow someone is to hang out with people who are also on the journey. Keep close to the people who are following the same person you are. Dorotheos of Gaza, a hermit from the Egyptian desert of the sixth century, spoke of discipleship as movement from the edge of a circle to its center. The closer one travels to the center, the more crowded the space becomes:

> Suppose we were to take a compass and insert the point and draw the outline of a circle. The center point is the same distance from any point on the circumference.... Let us suppose that this circle is the world and that God himself is the center: the straight lines drawn from the circumference to the center are the lives of human beings.... Let us assume for the sake of the analogy that to move toward God, then, human beings move from the circumference along the various radii of the circle to the center. But at the same time, the closer they are to God, the closer they become to one another; and the closer they are to one another, the closer they become to God.[5]

The Gospel of John begins with two birth narratives: the beginning of the cosmos and the beginning of discipleship. These two birth narratives may not work well for a Christmas pageant, but they map out the journey of discipleship. The first words of John's Jesus orient disciples to that journey through question, call, and invitation. In the next chapter, I want to look at some of the vivid characters the Gospel presents as traveling companions. As disciples focus on following, they walk shoulder to shoulder with these striking characters.

5. Dorotheos of Gaza, *Instructions* VI. "At the Wellspring of Faith," Taize Community. http://www.taize.fr/en_article5234.html.

CHAPTER 3

# Vivid Encounters:
# Meeting Jesus Meeting Others

BECAUSE HE RESISTED THE King of England's attempts to subordinate the church to the throne, Thomas Becket was murdered in the Canterbury Cathedral. Laid to rest where he died, Thomas was quickly canonized by Rome and declared a saint. For centuries pilgrims made the arduous journey to his shrine in the cathedral, walking there from all corners of England and the continent.

What did they seek? Some sought to honor the martyred archbishop; some sought miraculous cures; some sought release from heinous crimes; some simply sought adventures. Geoffrey Chaucer records the journey in *Canterbury Tales,* a masterpiece of Middle English. But in the end, *Canterbury Tales* is not about reaching the cathedral; it is not about honoring Thomas Becket. It's not about a place or a person. *Canterbury Tales* chronicles encounters with colorful characters who tell each other stories as they walk. After all, the way was long; the road, packed with other pilgrims. As readers listen to their stories, they too encounter a wild and crazy band of pilgrims, people who are just like them.

Like *Canterbury Tales,* John's is a crowded Gospel, populated with vivid characters, all of them drawn into the story of this strange man, Jesus. The Gospel doesn't so much *narrate* the life of Jesus as *enact* it. Narration reports from a seemingly objective third-person point of view: "They did this and then they did that.

Jesus said he was the bread of life, and the Pharisees groaned." Narration reads like a news story, and the report of a journalist can be read at a safe distance. In contrast, drama happens up front, in the moment, and in your face. There is direct speech: "Lord, what about him?" There is gesture: "He handed him over to them." There are complicated emotions: "I have told you already and you would not listen. Why do you want to hear it again? Do you also want to become his disciples?"

John presents the good news as opera, with the audience as the chorus. As action unfolds, character develops—and *characters* develop. They aren't just props stuck in the plot to make Jesus look good.

Eight of the twelve disciples get speaking parts, and the author identifies them by name: Simon Peter, Thomas, Philip, Judas Iscariot, another disciple named Judas, Andrew, Nathanael, and John, "the disciple whom Jesus loved." In addition to the disciples, important assisting roles are assigned to Mary, the mother of Jesus; Mary Magdalene, allegedly a "prostitute," but that was how men labeled any woman unattached to a man; Martha and Mary of Bethany, sisters of Lazarus; Greeks eager to meet Jesus; Pontius Pilate, the Roman prefect in Judea; unidentified Jews who believed in Jesus—and lots of unidentified Jews who didn't.

Stepping back from this crowd of people, what stands out is its diversity. According to the cultural norms of the world behind the text, Jesus talks a lot to people "outside his tent." He speaks with people who don't share his class, his status, his gender, his religion, his occupation, and his level of education. He speaks with people who fall outside the purity codes of Jewish religion: women, foreigners, non-Jews, people considered "unrighteous" by reason of physical disability, disease, poverty, or demonic possession. These people embody the audacious reach of Jesus' love. At the same time, contact with them puts him at risk of defilement. In itself, Jesus' choice of conversation partners gets him attention—even notoriety.

Moreover, no one can write off the conversations Jesus conducts with all these strange and amazing people as "small talk," something to fill in the blanks around major discourses. These conversations count as "big talk." In the world of the text, these conversations advance the plot and deliver John's argument about discipleship.

A few examples demonstrate John's strategy. Afraid to be seen by his peers speaking with Jesus, Nicodemus the Pharisee initially comes to Jesus at night (John 3:1–21). But later Nicodemus intervenes publicly to remind his fellow Pharisees that Jewish law requires a hearing before a conviction. He boldly accuses his colleagues of condemning Jesus without a trial (John 7:51). Nicodemus appears again at Jesus' burial, bearing myrrh and aloes for the ritual washing and embalming of bodies. Defying both Roman and Jewish authorities, he intends to give Jesus a proper Jewish burial (John 19:39). Initially fearful of the judgment of his colleagues, the Pharisee learns to push back against authority.

Mary Magdalene, not one of the original twelve apostles, is the first to encounter the risen Christ. She returns to tell the disciples "I have seen the Lord" (John 20:19), making her, at least in the world according to John, the first evangelist or "preacher of the good news." Jesus' dizzying range of encounters and conversation partners challenges the world in front of the text to be so bold.

Further, these vivid encounters feature characters that have hearts, minds, and mouths of their own. Some of them not only talk *to* Jesus, they talk *back*. A Samaritan woman gives Jesus some pushback on his request for water: "How is it that you, a Jew, ask a drink of me, a woman of Samaria?" (John 4:9). Some characters, like Nicodemus, engage Jesus in long conversation, peppering him with questions until they get an answer they can understand. Others express frustration with Jesus' love of metaphor. "Now you are speaking plainly, not in any figure of speech!" (John 16:30). Then, there's that aching exchange between Jesus and Peter: "Do you also wish to go away?" The disciples push right back with a question of their own: "Lord, to whom can we go?"(John 6:67–68). After all, Jesus' followers burned all their bridges and severed all their connections to follow Jesus—and he won't even tell them where he's going!

⌒

This chapter examines more closely the double edge of encounter in John's gospel, both the encounters it presents and the encounters it provokes. To explore the encounters the Gospel presents, we move into the world *of* the text, cataloguing the kinds of encounters in the Gospel. Then, to explore the encounters the Gospel provokes, we move into the world *in front of* the text, examining what happens when disciples today read Scripture for *encounter*, not just *information*.

## A Taxonomy of Encounters In The World Of The Text

In the world according to John, all of the encounters between Jesus and other people—and often among the people themselves—flow out of the Gospel's central question: "Who are you?" The encounters all address identity and in varying ways.

- One type of encounter treats Jesus' identity. Every one of the seven traditional "I AM" sayings and even the smaller, more incidental "I am" sayings are the direct result of encounters between Jesus and people who want to talk with him.

- Other encounters mutually identify both Jesus and the person he speaks with. There's even a negative example of this: In denying Jesus' identity in the courtyard of Caiaphas, Peter denies himself.

- Another class of encounters occur around miracles: "signs and wonders" that require some kind of explanation. There were lots of miracle-workers and magicians in the ancient world; Jesus wants to be certain he gives proper credit for his power.

- Finally, some encounters simply collapse into incomprehension. No amount of teaching and no kind of dazzle seems to dismantle people's preconceptions of who Jesus ought to be or how the Son of God ought to comport himself in the world.

## Encounters That Identify Jesus

Most often, encounters reveal some aspect of Jesus' identity. Early encounters between John the Baptist, his disciples, and Jesus point directly to him as "the Son of God" (John 1:34), "the Lamb of God" (John 1:35), and "the bridegroom" (John 3:29). At least John the Baptist knows who Jesus is. John the Baptist also knows who he himself is—and who he is *not*. Again and again, the Baptizer denies being the Messiah. He tells people he's not the bridegroom, but the bridegroom's "friend" (John 3:29); he's "the voice of one crying out in the wilderness," preparing the way for the Messiah (John 1:23; cf. Isa 40:3). John the Baptist knows that his role is almost over.

Encounter prompts all of the traditional "I AM" sayings in the Gospel. Here Jesus tells people directly who he is. These sayings may come in the middle of a longer discourse, but encounter sets the stage for all of them. For example, a miraculous feeding of 5,000 people with just five loaves of bread and two fish prompts Jesus to identify himself as "the bread of life" (John 6:35). Food is a basic human necessity. Jesus presents himself as the food these hungry people seek.

Then, the Festival of Booths featured the ritual lighting of great golden lamps in the Temple at Jerusalem. At the celebration, Jesus talks with Pharisees who want to nail down his identity. Their imagination only stretches as far as "prophet" or "Messiah," but they can't quite believe a Messiah would come from Galilee. In the midst of a hostile confrontation under these great lamps, Jesus identifies himself as "the light of the world" (John 8:12). It wasn't an answer anyone wanted to hear.[1]

An encounter with a man born blind occasions another confrontation with the religious leaders. As they witness a miraculous restoration of sight, they demand of Jesus directly: "Surely, we are not blind, are we?" (John 9:40). Jesus responds indirectly,

---

1. The conversation with the Pharisees during the Festival of the Booths at the Temple of Jerusalem is interrupted by the story of the woman caught in adultery (John 8:1–11).

proceeding to talk about sheep, animals that respond not to sight, but sound. They *hear* the shepherd's voice; moreover, they *recognize* the shepherd's voice. Sheep might as well be blind.

Jesus expands on this vivid metaphor of the shepherd. First, he identifies himself as "the gate" (John 10:9). In the ancient world, shepherds lay across the opening of square stone pens, using their bodies to block the entrance. Predators that wanted to get in and sheep that wanted to get out had to first get over or around the body of the shepherd. Then, Jesus identifies himself as "the Good Shepherd," whose sheep know his voice and whom he protects (John 10:11). The whole discourse implies that, even if the Pharisees are blind, they are not deaf and should be able to recognize the voice of a good shepherd in their midst. But the Pharisees prove themselves to be both blind and deaf to the divine mystery in their midst.

In conversation with Martha at the death of Lazarus, Jesus identifies himself as "the resurrection and the life." She responds with one of the clearest and most confident confessions of who Jesus really is: "Yes, Lord, I believe that you are the Messiah, the Son of God, the one coming into the world" (John 11:27). None of the disciples, who've been Jesus' constant companions, have seen his true identity with such clarity.

John's Jesus notices the disciples' cluelessness. The long "farewell discourse" (John 13–17) plays like the final class given by a frustrated teacher to a bunch of intractable students. Because Jesus intimated that he was going away, everyone wants to know where he's going, how to get there, and whether or not they can come along. Thomas asks for directions, to which Jesus replies: "I AM the way" (John 14:6). No one understands Jesus' answer. They want a destination.

Philip tries a different tack, asking Jesus to simply show them this "Father" he keeps talking to and about. Now Jesus is frustrated: "Have I been with you all this time . . . , and you still do not know me?" (John 14:9) If you've seen me, you've seen the Father, he tells them. Like the Pharisees, Jesus' own followers reveal themselves to be both blind and deaf.

Then Jesus tries a different strategy himself, drawing on a very concrete metaphor. This time he not only identifies himself —"I AM the vine"—he identifies the disciples as well: "YOU ARE the branches" (John 15:5). It's the first time he has identified the disciples in relationship to himself. He does this a second time, telling the disciples "YOU ARE my friends" (John 15:14). Moreover, he demonstrates that he is their friend, because he shows them that there is no greater love than "to lay down one's life for one's friends" (John 15:13).

Friendship, an important relationship in the Hellenistic context, deepens discipleship. Unlike today, where a friend is "someone who likes you," in the ancient world a friend was someone who told you the truth. The opposite of a friend, then, was not an enemy, but a "flatterer," someone who told you merely what you wanted to hear.

Here friendship delivers the truth in flesh and blood. Jesus reminds disciples:

> I do not call you servants any longer, because the servant does not know what the master is doing; but I have called you friends, because I have made known to you everything that I have heard from my Father. (John 15:15)

The disciples would prefer to be servants, because a servant merely does what he's told, nothing less, but also nothing more. Servants have to be told the master's wishes in any given situation. Disciples, in contrast, know too much. Disciples know the master's intention. They have the freedom and the responsibility to enact that intention in any given situation. Disciples know what to do without having to be told all the time.

An ordinary analogy opens up this distinction. When my sister and I were growing up, our parents told us how to behave in new situations. They also told us why we should behave that way. The rationale was dead simple: we were Stortz girls—and that's how Stortz girls behaved. That identity infused a certain pattern of behavior. It wasn't always the way our friends got to behave, but then, they weren't Stortz girls.

Over time, our parents expected us to internalize that pattern of behavior, so that we'd display "conduct becoming" for Stortz girls without having to be told what to do. Certain behaviors fit the profile; other behaviors were strictly off limits. This internalized behavior constituted "minding," as my mother put it. "Mind me," she'd say as we entered a grocery store.

Isn't this what the Apostle Paul talks about when he exhorts the community of Christians at Philippi to "mind Christ," displaying in their lives "conduct becoming" of Christians? Isn't that what Paul means in telling the Philippians to "be of the same *mind*, having the same love, being in full accord and of one *mind*" (Phil 2:2)? As Christians, he says, the pattern of Christ's life should shape their own lives.

Ah! Jesus' disciples clearly haven't registered all this wisdom, but his only hope before his death is that time, prayer, and the presence of the Spirit will activate their experience. He ends the final seminar with a long prayer for the disciples. It's clear they need it.

Under closer inspection, the long "farewell discourse" is not a fond farewell. There's tension in the room. A meal that should have been an occasion for people to come together for the Passover meal shows them shooting off like sparks. Philip demands to see Jesus' Father, and Jesus turns down the request. Thomas and Peter want to know where Jesus is going, and they dismiss his response. Judas can't even stay in the room but leaves to set in motion the awful juggernaut of events that leads to Jesus' execution. There's lots of tension in the room. But the friction of encounter prompts disclosure, as Jesus gives the disciples one last chance to see who he really is.

## Encounters that Mutually Identify Jesus and Someone Else

Sometimes revelation is mutual. People who encounter this strange and wonderful teacher not only get to know him but get to know themselves better. An encounter between Jesus and Nathanael generates mutual recognition. Jesus identifies Nathanael as "an

45

Israelite in whom there is no deceit!" and Nathanael suddenly sees someone from no-good Nazareth as "the Son of God and the King of Israel" (John 1:47–49). Later, Jesus tells a Samaritan woman her entire marital history. Then, she returns to her own people, telling them she has met the Messiah. When they come to see for themselves, they proclaim Jesus as "the savior of the world" (John 4:42). That "world" includes Samaritans, but the message comes out of a mutually revealing encounter between Jesus and a woman coming to draw water at a well.

The story of Peter at Jesus' trial offers a negative example of mutual revelation. This series of encounters erases identity. People in the high priest's courtyard pose to Peter the central question of the Gospel: "Who are you?" They want to know if he is one of Jesus' disciples. Three times Peter shuns the affiliation, saying again and again: "I am not" (John 18:25–27). There's a deliberate echo here to all of Jesus' "I AM" sayings, but now they roll out in negation. In denying Jesus, Peter denies himself.[2]

If the whole phenomenon of mutual identification seems remote, think of the signs people all over the world held up after the Paris shootings at the offices of Charlie Hebdo and in a kosher supermarket in Paris on January 7, 2015. Soon afterward there were signs in every language identifying *with* the murdered journalists by identifying *as* them: "*Je suis Charlie.*" "*Ich bin Charlie.*" "*Yo soy Charlie.*" People expressed their solidarity with the victims by identification.

Nor were the shootings the first or only expressions of mutual identification in recent years. After African American teenager Trayvon Martin was gunned down by George Zimmerman in a Florida gated community, people across the United States wore hoodies in memory of the hoodie Martin had on when he was

2. This comes just after Jesus' arrest in the garden, where the religious authorities come looking for him. Meeting them, Jesus asks the same question he asked at the beginning of John's account: "Whom are you looking for?" When the soldiers respond, he says simply and repeatedly: "I am he" (John 18:5, 6, 8; *ego eimi*). These simple statements, along with all the other "I AM" sayings, fuel the plot to eliminate him. But Jesus' willingness to embrace his identity at all costs contrasts sharply with Peter's denials.

shot. People further displayed their outrage by identification, an expression of solidarity that prompted Washington, DC-based photographer and activist Eunique Jones to chronicle that identification visually the way Chaucer chronicled stories of pilgrims headed to Canterbury.[3]

People identify *with* others by identifying *as* them.

## Encounters that Unpack "Signs and Wonders"

Sometimes miracles accompany encounters, because Jesus reveals his identity not simply in words but in actions. In one encounter, Jesus feeds thousands with nothing but a few fish, a few more loaves of bread, and a blessing. The crowds want to make him king (John 6:15). That is not who Jesus is, and he walks across the Sea of Galilee to get away from them. In another encounter, a blind man looks at things more clearly. Sight restored, he quite literally sees in Jesus "the Son of Man" (John 9:35). As noted, Jesus uses Lazarus's resurrection to name himself as the resurrection and the life. Miracles do double duty to reveal who Jesus really is as well as to heal, feed, and bring life out of death.

## Encounters that Frustrate

Finally, a few encounters end in utter frustration. Both John the Baptist and Jesus refuse the identities people project onto them, angering their interrogators and ensuring their deaths. Religious authorities eager to identify John the Baptist give him a limited range of options: Elijah, the prophet, or the Messiah. Pick one, they demand. John the Baptist steadfastly refuses each title.

---

3. Photographer Eunique Jones Gibson did a powerful series on identity and solidarity, focusing on police brutality in this country: *One Photo. One Hoodie. One Goal. Justice.* https://www.facebook.com/iamtrayvonmartinphotoawareness/info?tab=page_info.

For more on Eunique Jones Gibson, see her website: http://www.eunique-jones.com/.

In a replay of that initial encounter, Jesus appears before Pilate, who keeps trying to get clear on who this man is and what he's done that has so irritated the crowds. Pilate's entire interrogation revolves around the Gospel's central question: "Who are you?" He asks where Jesus is from, if he's King of the Jews, what he's done. Jesus turns the tables, putting Pilate on trial. He questions his interrogator: "Do you ask this on your own, or did others tell you about me?" When Jesus starts talking about "belonging to the truth," the Roman proconsul gives up: "What is truth?" In fact, truth stands in front of him, in the person of this man from Nazareth, as he told his own disciples in their final seminar: "I AM the way, and the truth, and the life" (John 14:6).

## Audience Participation: Engaging the World in Front of the Text

Whether they identify Jesus or identify both Jesus and the ones with whom he converses, whether they unpack "signs and wonders," whether they simply frustrate, these vivid encounters in John's gospel do more than describe the historical impact Jesus had. They engage disciples around the world and across the centuries. Simply and forcefully, the encounters of John's gospel encounter readers today. They do that by inviting them into the scene, by affecting their emotions, and finally, by deepening those emotions into steady dispositions.

### Inhabiting the Scene

The encounters of John's gospel don't simply report facts to passive readers. Rather, John's encounters invite audience participation, thrusting readers into the scene. For example, during the "farewell discourse," disciples pepper Jesus with questions. It's easy to list them: "Why can't you speak more clearly? Why must everything be couched in parables?" "Why do you have to go away?" "Where are you going?"

But John's gospel invites readers not only to enumerate the disciples' questions, but to *adopt* them. "Why can't *you* be clearer?" "Why do *you* have to go away?" "*Where* are you going?" "Why are *we* so clueless?!" The disciples' questions become their own.

Think of the layers of adoption displayed in a medieval altarpiece like the Portinari Altarpiece.[4]

The piece doesn't simply display a scene from the life of Jesus; it draws viewers into the scene, inviting them to address the question: What's going on? In the painting, the artist depicts the adoration of the magi, ancient astronomers who saw a new star in the sky and launched an exploration to answer their own question: What's going on? In the altarpiece, the magi kneel at the manger, along with shepherds on the ground and angels in the sky. In a wonderful compression of history, Mary Magdalene, St. Margaret, and St. Thomas also come to pay their respects to a Jesus they only meet as a grown-up. The artist puts his patron, Tommaso Portinari, in the artwork as well. Most striking is an empty space in front of manger, which is where contemporary spectators stand. Everyone gathers around a single question: What's going on? Gathering around the manger, viewers become worshipers like everyone else in the painting. No longer merely looking *at* the manger, worshipers look *with* the others. With its vivid characters, lifelike encounters, and sheer drama, John's encounters have a similar effect.

## Engaging the Emotions

Whether painted or narrated, encounters invite people *into* situations. Spectators become worshipers; readers become participants. They *experience* what's going on. Surrounded by action, jostled by these lifelike characters, we find ourselves emotionally engaged, and emotions like empathy and compassion function as the connective tissue in the body politic.

Because John's characters are so sharply drawn, readers cannot help but respond to them emotionally. We admire the Samaritan

4. Hugo van der Goes, *The Portinari Altarpiece*, c. 1475. http://www.wga.hu/tours/flemish/goes/index1.html.

woman's spunk and candor, but we also learn from her encounter with Jesus that he welcomes feistiness. We're encouraged to follow her example. We weep with Mary when we sense God's absence in our own lives in the familiar ways that we've come to rely on. But we also learn from her that the risen Christ will find us again if we simply pay attention and erase all expectations of how we think that should happen. We despair of Peter's impetuousness, but we also share his impatience. Moreover, we further learn from Peter's experience that even betrayal, which is *the* sin in friendship, doesn't disqualify disciples. If Peter didn't get thrown off the discipleship bus, we won't be cast out either.

## Patterning the Emotions

Love is the answer, regardless of the question.

If I had a graphic that captured the way most people in my first-world, mainstream Protestant communions talk about God, it would be a smiling yellow face: no sadness, but also no real joy; no judgment, but also no real depth. People assume God likes them; they take God's forgiveness for granted. John's radical proclamation that God is *love* flattens to the generic affability: God is "*like.*"

Entering encounters in John's gospel and experiencing within ourselves the emotions they evoke, we marvel at their range. Fear, exasperation, surprise, delight, scorn, despair, over-the-top enthusiasm, deep joy: nothing seems off limits to the Word made flesh. People dress up for church on Sunday, but there's no need to dress up for Jesus emotionally. John's Jesus absorbs the full range of human emotions, positive, negative, and everything in between. All emotions are welcome, and there's only one set divine response. John's Jesus simply responds with love, nothing more and nothing less.

Against that horizon of love, these other emotions move, roll, and even pound, like waves on the shore. There's spume and spray, riptides and undertow, but far out at sea, the horizon remains invariant, a single line marking the boundary between water and sky. In John's gospel, the steady horizon is love, rendering all the other emotions like the restlessness of the waves. They build with power, but once they break, they flow back into the vastness of the ocean.

By responding to their every emotion with unfailing love, Jesus tries to teach disciples how to love. He absorbs all of the disciples' emotions, positive and negative, and returns them to the disciples as love. Jesus hopes receiving love will encourage them to give it. It shouldn't depend on what they had for breakfast or how they're feeling that day. Jesus wants love to be so deeply engrained in his disciples that they will respond in every situation with love. Or in the words of the pop song, "Love is the answer"—no matter what the question, no matter what the circumstance.

Jesus asks for only love in return, but it's a radical request: "Love one another, as I have loved you" (John 13:34, 15:12). We hear this so often, it's hard to register its force. Humans yearn to love and to be loved, in impossibly equal amounts. If we were honest, we would confess to wanting every declaration of love to be answered with an immediate response: "I love you too." We want at least an equal return on our emotional investment.

But Jesus didn't say "love *me*, as I have loved you." He doesn't even say "love *God*, as I have loved you." He demands neither reciprocity nor piety. Instead, he urges disciples to be abundant, even reckless, in loving: "Love *one another*, as I have loved you." To paraphrase: Remember how I responded to every emotion you presented to me—your fears, your exasperation, your despair, your delights, your joys, and your sorrows. I simply responded with love. Whatever emotion is thrown at you, always respond in love. Jesus doesn't need for us to love him—or even God; he needs us to love one another.

The final conversation between Jesus and Peter repeats the "new commandment" in a way that is powerfully particular to Peter. After all, Peter betrays Jesus three times, and three times Jesus asks him: "Do you love me?" Three times Peter responds with the answer of reciprocity: "Yes, I love you." But reciprocity isn't enough. Jesus doesn't want "payback," he wants Peter to "pay love forward." He demands that Peter "feed my lambs," "tend my sheep," and "feed my sheep." Scholars spill ink over the distinctions between "feeding" and "tending," between "sheep" and "lambs." But each command is just another way of reminding Peter to "love one another," this time uttered in a way that is unique to Peter's particular history with Jesus. Each declaration of love erases one of his betrayals of Jesus in the courtyard of the high priest.

"Love one another as I have loved you." In a final conversation with his most impetuous disciples, Jesus gives Peter specific instruction. How do we hear that instruction in our own lives against the background of our own particular history with Jesus?

## Conclusion

Prayer invites disciples to encounter God whenever disciples need to and wherever they are. It's a way of fine-tuning the capacity for encounter, which involves honest conversation. One man described his journey: "First, I began to pray by talking *at* God, the way I'd talk *at* someone on an airplane or in a checkout line. Then, as I began to get a sense of God's presence, I talked *to* God. And gradually, I began talking *with* God as one would speak with a trusted friend. Now, I find myself listening *to* God, as God speaks through Scripture or nature or the people around me. And more often, I'm listening *for* God, combing the silences for God's presence."

# CHAPTER 4

# Provocative Questions:
# The Spark of Encounter

A STUDENT WALKED INTO my office in Minneapolis, distraught. She had the opportunity to take an internship in Washington, DC for the spring semester. Now, in the city in which we were sitting on that fall afternoon, watching golden mountain ash leaves swirl outside in the wind, her grandmother was dying. "What should I do?" she asked. We talked into the late afternoon, outlining possible options.

Then I posed another question: "Where's the invitation in all of this?" I had no answers; I simply reframed the question. Instead of asking *what to do*, I asked *what was going on*; instead of *acting*, she had to *respond*. Reframing the question didn't make things any easier for her, but it gave her a different angle of vision. She needed that. Sometimes asking the right question is more important than coming up with an answer to the wrong one.

Nineteenth-century German poet Rainer Marie Rilke advised a young poet to "live the questions":

> Be patient toward all that is unsolved in your heart and try to love the questions themselves, as if they were locked rooms or books written in a very foreign language. . . . Don't search for the answers, which could not be given to you now, because you would not be able to live them. And the point is, to live everything. Live the questions now. Perhaps then someday, far in the future

you will gradually, without even noticing it, live into the
answer.[1]

⤳

In this chapter, we look at questions from John and Genesis,
viewing them through the lens of the dilemma described above,
then broadening the view to see how these questions might direct
disciples today. We begin with the Socratic Jesus of John's gospel.
Not only does Jesus call his disciples with a question, but in John's
gospel he leads them with questions throughout. Like Son, like
Father: Genesis's creation stories reveal a Socratic God, one who
also leads with questions. All of these questions demand attention
as followers make the journey of discipleship today.

## A Socratic Jesus

In John's gospel, the first words out of Jesus' mouth pose a question:
"What are you looking for?"(John 1:38). This question inaugurates
Jesus' entire ministry. He could have launched it differently. He
could have given orders; he could have made a recruitment effort.
Instead, he begins with a simple question: "What are you looking
for?"

It doesn't matter how disciples answer; it matters only that
they follow him. But Jesus has certainly posed the right question.
Not surprisingly, the Gospel concludes with Jesus posing another
question, this one repeated three times: "Do you love me?"[2] Questions begin and end the journey of discipleship; questions guide
it along the way. Jesus leads the disciples not by command, but by
questions.

Often, this Socratic Jesus responds to a question not with an
answer, but with another question. Early in the story, when Jesus
encounters him under a shade tree teaching disciples of his own,

1. Rilke, *Letters to a Young Poet*. Also available at http://carrothers.com/
rilke4.htm

2. John 21:15, 16, 17.

Nathanael asks Jesus: "Where did you get to know me?" (John 1:48). Jesus counters with a question: "Do you believe because I told you that I saw you under the fig tree?" (John 1:50).

Sometimes questions prompt revelation. Jesus tells Martha that no one who believes in him will ever die, and then he asks her directly: "Do you believe this?" The answer Martha gives makes her one of the first evangelists: "I believe that you are the Messiah, the Son of God, the one coming into the world" (John 11:27).

Sometimes questions prompt healing. Jesus asks a lame man at the pool of Bethzatha: "Do you want to be made well?" (John 5:6). Assuming nothing, Jesus simply asks the man what *he* wants.

Sometimes Jesus puts into words a question that is unspoken but on everyone's mind. In John's account of a miraculous feeding, Jesus asks: "Where are we to buy bread for these people to eat?" (John 6:5).[3] The Synoptic Gospels put the question in the disciples' mouths. It's something everyone is wondering.

Sometimes someone else speaks the unspeakable question, as Pilate does before Jesus at his trial. "What is truth?" he asks (John 18:38). Truth stands before him, and he can't see it.

Sometimes the question Jesus poses has no answer, as when he disperses a crowd ready to stone a woman convicted of adultery. "Woman, where are they? Has no one condemned you?" (John 8:10).

John's Jesus asks lots of questions.

## A Socratic God

Jesus' love of questions should not be surprising. His father in heaven has the same penchant. Consider the questions scattered throughout the first chapters of the story of the first creation in Genesis: "Where are you?" "What have you done?" "Who told you that?" "Why are you angry?" "Where is your brother?" Once noticed, these questions stick in the reader's brain like burrs. They

---

3. Look at the other Synoptic accounts of this miraculous feeding from Matthew 14:13–21; Mark 6:32–44; and Luke 9:10–17.

don't so much tell you what to do as help you pay attention to what's being done.

Questions organize the operating manual for a new creation, whether God in creation is fashioning the earth and all that is in it or whether God in Jesus is forming disciples. In the stories of creation in Genesis and in John, creatures encounter a God who's always asking questions, and those questions reframe the world.

## Living the Questions from the First Creation

### *"Adam, where are you?" (Gen 3:9)*

Adam used to walk in the garden in the cool of the evening and talk with God. After the fateful encounter with the forbidden fruit, though, he hides himself. God asks about his absence. The question addresses our location in front of the text. Where are you physically? Where are you emotionally? Where are you spiritually?

Posing this question to my student would have invited her to locate herself in relationship to her family and her community, her career and her calling. Where was the "moral tug" in all of these relationships?

### *"Who told you that?" (Gen 3:11)*

Adam answers God's first question by referring to his nakedness. God then asks Adam how the notion of "nakedness" entered his consciousness in the first place. The story reveals a shame about physical exposure, but Adam also wants to hide his naked desire to play God all by himself.

The question addresses us the world in front of the text to ask what scripts we live by, the ones that tell us what to buy and where, what to do and with whom, where to go and how often. The question invites disciples to discern what's worthwhile and what's simply white noise.

Posing this question to my student would have invited her to consider what scripts she was living out of: Who authored them?

Which should she pay more and less attention to? What story was *she* authoring?

### *"What have you done?" (Gen 3:13)*

God asks Adam to give an account of what happened with the forbidden fruit. When pressed to tell the story in his own words, he resorts to blame, blaming the snake, blaming Eve, even blaming God for creating her: "That woman whom you gave me . . ." (Gen 3:12). He tries to shake off all responsibility.

The question asks us in front of the text for an honest accounting, noting good things and bad, gifts and liabilities. Posing this question to my student would have invited her to look at all that she "had done, O Lord, and left undone," in the words of an ancient prayer of confession, both good things and not-so-good.[4] But this account moves beyond the balance sheet to ask about the person behind these good deeds and bad. Who is she? And who does she aspire to be? How might that aspiration inform the present?[5]

### *"Why are you angry?" (Gen 4:6)*

God poses this question to Cain, the son of Adam and Eve, who felt that God had favored the grain offering of his brother Abel

---

4. The language is from the *Confiteor* of the Roman Rite Mass, which roughly translates as "I confess to almighty God, and to you, my brothers and sisters, that I have greatly sinned in my thoughts and in my words, in what I have done, and in what I have failed to do; through my fault, through my fault, through my most grievous fault. Therefore, I ask blessed Mary, ever virgin, all the angels and saints, and you, my brothers and sisters, to pray for me to the Lord our God."

5. No one wants to be judged by his worst actions, and people are more than the sum of their deeds, both good ones and bad. But action shapes character. When a student identified himself as "a truthful person, but every now and then I tell a little white lie," I countered: "But doesn't that make you a little white liar?" There was no response. Character is what we do when no one is looking.

and spurned for his meat offering. In so many eruptions of rage, fear provokes anger, and fear is the issue here. Cain fears his offering is not as good as his brother's. The question God poses asks us in front of the text to identify our fears, even befriend them. Anger can never be addressed if its underlying fear remains buried. Sometimes fear is worth naming publicly; always fear is worth knowing.

I wish I'd asked my student what she was afraid of. She needed the answer.

### *"Where is your brother?" (Gen 4:9)*

Again, God addresses Cain. Driven by fear and rage, Cain killed Abel. God noticed the absence. The story captures that secret longing of siblings to be "the only begotten son—or daughter" and treasured above all else. To the world in front of the text, the question raises the issue of otherness, how it's defined, how it's dealt with, whether it's even acknowledged. The question invites us to consider the other—whether grandmother, partner, friend, or potential client, whether Christian, Jew, or Muslim—and to name the other as "neighbor."

"Neighbor" is the biblical word for the "other." It carries the weight of the common space that neighbors share, a neighborhood, and the common good that neighbors pursue, the maintenance of a commons. Posing this question to my student would have invited her to step into the neighborhood and recognize that she isn't the only one acting or deciding. Whatever she does or doesn't do takes place in a community of agents.

Leading questions like the ones from the creation account of Genesis orient disciples to a complex world of action and character. Questions like these don't so much tell us what to do as acknowledge the complexity of the arena in which we act. Whether the questions have answers or not, they are the right questions to pose.

## Living the Questions from the Creation of Discipleship

Like Father, like Son. Questions drive the Genesis story of the creation. They also drive John's story of the creation of discipleship. Disciples are invited to "live the questions" that animate encounters along the way: "Who are you?" "What/whom are you looking for?" "Where do you dwell?" "What do you want me to do for you?" "Do you love me?" Questions like these become a kind of operating manual for disciples, helping them navigate the journey ahead.

### *"Who are you?" (John 1:19, 1:22, 8:25)*

John's creation story begins with a question that animates the entire Gospel, "Who are you?" In addressing that question, disciples find out who Jesus is and discover who they are along the way. All of the "I AM" sayings address this question, as Jesus reveals himself to the disciples.

But the identity of the master shapes the identity of disciples: "You are whom you follow!" Again and again, disciples are asked to whom they belong. Few answer with the clarity that possessed the Apostle Paul, "You belong to Christ, and Christ belongs to God" (1 Cor 3:23). For example, in denying he even knows Jesus, the Apostle Peter denies himself. If he doesn't know *whose* he is, Peter does not know *who* he is.

Peter's confusion at the end of the Gospel contrasts sharply with John the Baptist's repeated denials at its beginning. The Baptizer knows *who* and *whose* he is. He displays enviable insight into his identity. He is the friend of the bridegroom, not the bridegroom; the preparer of the way, not the Way itself; the "voice of one crying in the wilderness," not the Messiah himself.

Posed to my student this question would have helped her think about her own emerging place in the world, *who* she is. She could also think about the various communities that claim her, *whose* she is. Once she names them, she can begin to assess the legitimacy of their claims. Shifts in belonging trigger shifts in identity. She finds herself at a point developmentally and circumstantially where everything is in transition.

### *"What are you looking for?" (John 1:38; cf. 18:4, 7)*

The first words out of Jesus' mouth pose a question to two disciples of John the Baptist. They never answer Jesus' question, but respond instead with one of their own: "Where are you staying?"

Perhaps because he gets no answer, Jesus reframes the question throughout the Gospel. At his arrest, Jesus asks: "Whom are you looking for?" (John 18:4, 7). When the soldiers reply that they seek Jesus of Nazareth, he responds with the answer God gave Moses from the burning bush: "I AM" (John 18:6, *ego eimi*).[6] Familiar with the Mosaic context, the soldiers fall to the ground. Jesus asks again: "Whom are you looking for?" When the soldiers reply that they seek Jesus of Nazareth, he blunts the shock of his original answer: "I told you I AM he. So if you are looking for me, let these men go" (John 18:8). The soldiers arrest him. By asking the question a second time, Jesus seals his fate. He delivers himself up into the hands of the Jewish authorities.

Jesus asks the question a third time of Mary Magdalene, who is weeping outside an empty tomb. "Whom are you looking for?" She wants the old Jesus back again, and she doesn't recognize the risen Christ in front of her. It's only when he speaks that she recognizes her friend. Just as sheep recognize the voice of the shepherd, Mary recognizes the voice of her Lord. The vivid comparison between discipleship and shepherding occurs only in John. Sheep don't need to see in order to follow; they need only to hear.

It's significant that the question comes in two forms in John's gospel: "*What* are you looking for?" and "*Whom* are you looking for?" Sometimes people seek some*thing* when they're really

---

6. Some sources say "I am he;" others simply state "I AM," a direct reference to Moses's encounter with God in the burning bush (Exod 3:14). The soldiers' respond by falling to the ground, a move appropriate to the latter response.

looking for some*one*. The distinction between a thing and a person is important.

I wish I could have summoned this distinction between some *thing* and some *one* for my student. On the surface, she weighed some*thing*, an internship in Washington, against some*one*, her grandmother. She wanted to know what to do. In fact, the two choices were incomparable. One was a thing; one was a person. She could have recalibrated the dilemma differently: one involving two personal responsibilities, one to herself and the other to her grandmother. Whom should she choose? Both were significant.

## *"Do you want to be made well?" (John 5:6)*

Jesus asks a lame man at the pool of Bethzatha: "Do you want to be made well?" Jesus doesn't assume anything, even that a crippled man might want to walk. He simply asks the man what *he* wants, and he asks the man to put it in his own words, uncluttered by anyone else's assumptions. The man wants only to be put into the water when the surface begins to stir because the first person in the water after that agitation is healed. Someone else always beat him into the water.

Interestingly, Jesus doesn't do what the lame man wants. Jesus gives the man what he doesn't dare ask for: healing. "What do you want me to do?" Addressing this question involves both dependence and risk.

First, the question is an invitation to be needy in a world that values independence. It's a necessary invitation, because we can't intuit the wants and needs of another. How often partners or parents tell another partner or a child: "You have to tell me what you want from me: I can't read your mind." The question invites people to put into words what they want and need from someone else. When that someone else is God, the question prompts prayer.

Prayer invites disciples to put their needs into words and bring them before God. "Ask, and it will be given to you; search, and you will find; knock, and the door will be open to you" (Matt 7:7–8; cf. Luke 11:10). Ask, simply ask.

But doesn't God already know what disciples want? It's a good question, but maybe asking it is as much for their benefit as God's. They need to put into words their deepest yearnings—and be needy before God.

Second, addressing the question—"Do you want to be made well?"—takes big risks. After all, there's risk whenever people put their needs out there. They might get turned down. But they also might get turned *around*. "Every prayer is answered," a wise priest offered. Then he paused: "It just isn't answered the way we think it should be." Jesus didn't say "everyone who asks gets what they ask for." He said: "Everyone who asks receives." The act of asking primes people for receiving.

In the world according to John, when people ask for what they need, the desires themselves get altered. The lame man actually only asks to be the first one in the water. That's all he wants. Instead, he gets to walk again. At the empty tomb, Mary Magdalene asks only for the dead body of Jesus. That's all she wants. Instead, she gets the risen Christ. Back in their old lives after the crucifixion, the disciples want only to catch fish again. That's all they want. Instead, they get their risen Lord on the beach cooking them breakfast. In the biblical world, asking for what they want puts disciples in that dangerous position of having their desires themselves utterly transformed into what they need.

Transformation isn't always welcome. People worship what's familiar; they build shrines to their longings. As twentieth-century poet W. H. Auden remarked, "We would rather be ruined than changed."[7] But for all who dare to change, for all who put their longings out there, Jesus promises to "make all things new."

"What do you want me to do for you?" I wish I'd asked my student this question. It might have been helpful for both of us to have her say what she needed, rather than my intuiting it. Similarly, it might have been helpful for her to ask her family what they needed from her. There could have been surprises. On yet another level, it might have been helpful to have her ask God for what she

---

7. Auden, *The Age of Anxiety*, 105.

needed. Prayer would have put her in a posture to receive whatever happened as an "answer to prayer."

## "What is truth?" (John 18:38).

This question is asked *of* Jesus, not by him. Moreover, the question is asked by someone who stands as an "enemy" to the Jews, to the whole Jesus movement, and to the angry crowds demanding Jesus' death. This "enemy" actually wants to give Jesus a fair trial. Used to trying criminals and murderers, Pilate can't understand what this man has done wrong. When Jesus reports that his only "crime" is testifying to the truth, Pilate responds: "What is truth?" The inflection behind Pilate's question remains unclear. What is clear, though, is that the angry crowd in front of Pilate outnumbered the Romans and demanded sacrifice—and not just any sacrifice, but the sacrifice of Jesus. Only the Romans possessed the power to put someone to death.

What *is* truth? It's a question more suited to a classroom than a courtroom. A courtroom simply demands that *the* truth be told without delving into its nature. Pilate looks for just such an explanation of the facts at hand, but truth stands in front of him. He can't see it, because he isn't looking for it to come to him as a person.

Too often, the truth comes packaged in a creed or confession, where it can be memorized and repeated. Too often, the truth comes bound between the pages of a book, where it can be codified and enforced. Too often, the truth explains, distinguishes, and then sums up. All that can be taught.

But when truth comes as a person, the only thing left to do is follow that person wherever he goes. Maybe the whole encounter with Pilate aims to give the Roman proconsul a last chance to become a disciple himself.

I wish I'd posed this question "What is truth?" to my student. I would make her attend to the way that truth comes with skin. That is, truth comes in the person of people like her grandmother, her family, her teachers, her potential employers, even and especially the skin of her own body. More fluid and vulnerable than confessional, legal, or procedural truths, personal truth is also more flexible. Particularly when personal truth is tutored by the truth that comes as Jesus, personal truth moves from being solipsism into solidarity. If my student could find the traces of incarnation in her own situation, she might have a truth that she could live into and not simply lock down.[8]

## "Do you love me?" (John 21:15, 16, 17)

If truth comes to us as a series of propositions, the proper response is assent. Check the right box to agree to the terms and conditions of use. If truth comes to us as a creed, the proper relationship is belief, as believers who have a creed demonstrate when they recite it: "I believe in one God . . ."[9] But if the truth comes to us as a person, the most appropriate response is love.

Jesus's question to Peter closes out John's gospel. He asks the question of a disciple who betrayed him three times, and he repeats it three times. Three times Peter answers in the affirmative. The repetition "hurts" him, as the text notes, but each question forgives a betrayal. Peter gets a second chance. If there's hope for Peter, maybe there's hope for all the other disciples.

"Do you love me?" The exchange between Jesus and Peter is awkward, not only for the repetition but also for the substance of what's said. The conversation in Greek treats two different kinds of love: the love of friendship, *philia*, and the unconditional love of *agape*. The first two times that Jesus asks his question using the word for unconditional love, "Do you love (*agapas*) me?" Peter responds in terms of friendship: "Yes, you know that I love (*philo*) you." It's as if a lover asked the beloved: "Do you love me?" only to

8. E.g., Augustine's *vestigia trinitatis* and Justin Martyr's *logos spermatikos* were understandings of an indwelling truth.

9. Some Christian denominations, particularly those that grew out of the Radical Reformation, do not profess creeds, i.e., Church of the Brethren, Disciples of Christ, Unitarian Universalist, Quakers, et al. They believe that to try to make God fit into the constraints of human language is blasphemous.

have the beloved respond: "You know I really, really *like* you." This happens twice. Clearly, Jesus and this disciple are not on the same wavelength.

Then, grace breaks into a conversation going nowhere: Jesus adjusts his question to match Peter's response. The last time he poses his question to Peter, Jesus draws on the only terms Peter can handle: "Do you love (*phileis*) me?" as in, "Do you really, really like me?" This time Peter's response mirrors the question. There's finally symmetry. Jesus ends this extraordinary encounter by repeating to Peter the invitation of discipleship: "Follow me."

Jesus discussed love at length with his disciples in his final discourse with them (John 13—17). In the course of this conversation and in the context of a foot washing, he called them "friends," rather than "slaves," but he spoke of the relationship in terms of the unconditional love of *agape*. The disciples registered the relationship, but not its content. As the coach told a lazy quarterback: "You want the position without putting in all the work." The work of being a Jesus' "friend" is learning to love unconditionally and indiscriminately.

An old hymn marvels "What a friend we have in Jesus" but look at the friends Jesus has! He seems to have expansive tastes. He shows solidarity with the poor, but spends time with rich friends in Bethany, like Mary, Martha, and Lazarus. He argues with the Pharisees, but then talks to Rabbi Nicodemus at night. He invites tax collectors onto the discipleship bus, and they were among the most despised people to Jews under Roman occupation. He hangs out with alleged "prostitutes" and widows, both of them free radicals socially, because they were not under protection of a man. He consorts with broken, diseased, and bleeding people who would have ritually defiled a "righteous" Jew. Jesus loved the most dangerous and unlovable kinds of people. Furthermore, they are people who would definitely not have loved—or even liked—each other.

"Do you love me?" Behind that question is another: "Can you love the way I love?" "Can you love the people I do?" "Can you love what is unlovely—even when it shows up inside yourself or your community?" Peter's frustration with Jesus' questioning covers his inability to love the way Jesus loves. He can't even love himself the way Jesus loves him. Jesus has forgiven him, but can he forgive himself?

I could imagine this question—"Do you love me?"—being posed to my student by her grandmother, by her family, even to herself. As Peter found, it's a loaded question—with a "loaded" answer as well. Yet both question and answer broker forgiveness. Whatever she decides, however she responds, my young friend will need forgiveness. No course of action short of cloning herself and being in two places simultaneously meets the demands of her dilemma. But forgiveness allows people to live in past imperfect tense, rather than past perfect tense. There is no right answer to her question, "What should I do?" But forgiveness invites her to live the questions—and to keep asking them.

## Conclusion

My student asked a question: "What should I do?" only to find another question: "Where's the invitation in all of this?" The question reframed the situation and challenged her to pose additional questions of her own.

These leading questions from John and Genesis might be helpful for anyone discerning a path or an invitation, whether they are outside or inside the traditions from which they came. But for someone within the Judaeo-Christian tradition these questions have added traction. They point toward a God who values questions and leads by asking them. God may or may not have all the right answers—but God certainly has the right questions, and the point, as Rilke suggests, is to "live them."

More importantly, these leading questions from Genesis and John offer an encounter with someone who promises to quest along with us. In John's gospel this is no one else than the Son of God, a Socratic Jesus. He begins his ministry with a question: "What are you looking for?" He closes it out with another question: "Do you love me?" He follows each question with an invitation to follow.

Who is the one whom we follow? It's to that question that we turn in the next chapter with a more careful study of the seven sayings in which Jesus reveals himself to disciples then—and now.

CHAPTER 5

# Identity Matters: Who Are You?

"WHO ARE YOU?" I pose this question to my students on the first day of each class. We make name tents. On the outside, in letters large enough to be seen from across the room, we print the names we'd like to be known by for the rest of the semester. On the inside, I ask them to answer three questions:

- "Who does the registrar think you are?"—because sometimes the official class roster doesn't match how students prefer to be addressed.

- "What's one thing you're really good at?"—because I want students to know they have gifts.

- Finally, "what's one community that needs you to be good at that?"—because communities confirm the gifts they have. A young Somali Muslim identified his gift as cooking, then explained proudly: "People want me to cook for all the family gatherings." A student athlete named wrestling. His team needed that gift, particularly in his weight class.

Shortly after January 7, 2015, people around the world started holding name tents in front of the media. These name tents expressed solidarity for victims of the shootings at the offices of the French magazine *Charlie Hebdo,* and a Jewish supermarket in Paris. In protest, Parisians took to the streets, showing their solidarity with signs that proclaimed "*Je suis Charlie*"—"I am Charlie."

In one group, a man wearing the white cap of a pilgrim from the *Hajj*,[1] carried a sign that said "*Je suis Juif*," "I am a Jew."

⥲

Identity matters. It did for Jesus. John's gospel doesn't shy away from dangerous answers. "Who are you?" The question opens the Gospel (John 1:19). There, as people try to identify Jesus, their attempts uncovered their own deep longings. Some yearned for a revolutionary hero; others sought a miracle worker; still others, the leader of a mystical sect. Even the people who joined up with Jesus didn't quite understand *what* they were getting into or *who* they were getting down with.

In this chapter, we look at how all of the Gospels address the question "Who are you?" in order to understand John's unique response. Disciples didn't recognize who Jesus was when he was with them. They had an even harder time recognizing the risen Christ. How would they recognize the spirit of the risen Christ after Jesus ascended to his Father?

Of all the Gospels, John's reckons with the question of identity. It does so in a series of unique "I AM" sayings that help disciples then and now find the spirit of the risen Christ in the midst of all the other spirits competing for their attention. John's sayings are distinctive among biblical narratives of recognition. As disciples identify Jesus more fully, they better understand themselves. Further, they find in him answer to their deepest longings.

## Biblical Narratives of Recognition

Among the biblical narratives of recognition, John's is distinctive.

The earliest Gospel, Mark, begins, not with a birth narrative, but with Jesus' baptism, the beginning of his public ministry. From there, the narrative careens to the crucifixion. It ends with

---

1. The *Hajj* is the pilgrimage to Mecca, one of the five pillars of Islam. Devout Muslims try to do it once in a lifetime.

the women running in terror from an empty tomb, "for they were afraid" (Mark 16:8).

Matthew's gospel takes time to teach, because people needed it. Attentive to Jesus' Jewish background and audience, Matthew presents Jesus as a rabbi who embodies the new law. People had to learn the difference between following the commandments of Torah and following a person.

The author of Luke-Acts assumes the role of armchair theologian, presenting "an orderly account" that covers the earthly life of Jesus, his death and resurrection, and concludes with the ongoing work of his spirit among the earliest communities. Luke-Acts tells the "acts of the Spirit."

Historically, John's gospel comes last. As we have seen, it begins not with Jesus' baptism or birth but the birth of the cosmos. Consciously calling to mind Genesis, John narrates a new creation, the creation of disciples. The work of that creation continues to this day through the spirit of the risen Christ. John's task is to help people see that spirit.

The question for disciples then and now is: How can we encounter the spirit of the risen Christ? In a series of arresting "I AM" sayings unique to the Gospel, John tells us where to look. For the journey that discipleship demands, followers don't need maps or directions; they simply need *someone*. They'd better be able to recognize him.

### Recognizing Jesus: The Synoptic Gospels' Answer

People had a hard time figuring out who Jesus was even when he was with them. Suspecting perhaps he cannot be seen for who he really is, Jesus asks the disciples who people think he really is. In the Synoptic Gospels, he takes the temperature of the crowds following him first: "Who do people say that I am?" (Mark 8:27–35; Matt 16:13–23; Luke 9:18–22). The disciples respond with a list of the usual suspects: Elijah, John the Baptist, or one of the prophets. Their answers replay the temptation in the wilderness, but they also reflect the crowd's deepest desires.

## The Temptation

In the wilderness temptations (Matt 4:1–11, Luke 4:1–13, and in a condensed version, Mark 1:12–13), Satan dares Jesus to throw himself off the pinnacle of the Temple at Jerusalem, tempting him to fly or float to the ground. He refuses, denying he is Elijah. According to Jewish legend, Elijah would appear in the Temple heights just before the day of liberation. If Jesus were Elijah, that day of liberation would have arrived. The crowd longs for liberation.

In another scene, Satan dares Jesus to turn stones into loaves of bread, just like Moses, the greatest of the prophets, who brought water from rocks and bread from heaven. Again, Jesus refuses, denying that he is Moses. But if he were Moses, hungry people would be fed. The crowd longs for physical and spiritual food.

In another scene, Satan dares Jesus to worship him in exchange for all the kingdoms of the world. A third time, Jesus refuses, denying that he is a worldly ruler. But if he were king, Jews would share in that power, evidence that they were indeed God's "chosen people." The crowd longs for return of the "promised land" to the people of the promise.

## The Interrogation Scene

All three synoptic gospels replay the wilderness temptations in a kind of Q&A that Jesus conducts with his disciples (Mark 8:27–33, Matt 16:13–23, Luke 9:18–22) midway through his ministry. The question "Who do people say that I am?" organizes the interrogation, only now the tempter is not Satan, but the disciples themselves. At first, they simply report what they've heard people saying about Jesus: "John the Baptist; and others; Elijah, and still others, one of the prophets" (Mark 8:27–28).

But these are precisely the roles Jesus refused. In the wilderness they were Satan's suggestions. Now Jesus' followers put them forth, offering him a second temptation. But they also reveal their own deepest longings. They long for liberation, for food, for favor.

When Jesus turns the question directly to his disciples, these people who know him best do no better than the crowds. Peter identifies him as the "Messiah" (Mark 8:29; cf. Matt 16:16; Luke 9:20).

The Jewish "Messiah" was supposed to be a revolutionary hero who would liberate God's chosen people from foreign occupation. If Jesus were that kind of Messiah, then the disciples would be the guerrilla troops in charge of the resistance. Peter longs to be a general in the army of liberation.

This is not the right answer, and in all of the accounts, Jesus responds by warning the disciples to tell no one (Mark 8:30; cf. Matt 16:20; Luke 9:21). He concludes this Q&A by talking about a "Son of Man" who suffers injustice, not a warrior who fights against it.

## Recognizing Jesus: John's Answer

John helps disciples discern the spirits. The "I AM" sayings tell disciples then and now how to recognize the spirit of Christ and how to distinguish that spirit from all the other spirits out there.

The fourth Gospel briefly dispenses with temptation and interrogation scenes in its first chapter. Jewish leaders approach John the Baptist to pose to him the wilderness temptation questions. They ask him directly if he is Elijah, the "prophet" (the greatest of whom was Moses), or the Messiah, all of whom feature in the Synoptic Gospels' wilderness temptation and interrogation scenes. John the Baptist denies he is the one they're looking for. Here the questions themselves register the confusion about Jesus and John; the questions telegraph the deepest longings of the people.

When Jesus arrives, John the Baptist identifies him as the "lamb of God," a sacrificial animal in Jewish ritual. John's version of the temptation scene presents all of its key elements in characteristic fashion. Everything is in terms of identity.

Jesus takes the story from there. In the rest of the Gospel, he identifies himself directly in a series of sayings found only in John's gospel. As noted in the prior chapters, the "I AM" statements always arise out of encounters. Jesus corrects the vision of the people around him, in order that they may see him more sharply, as well as themselves.

## *"I AM the bread of life" (John 6:35)*

This saying occurs after John's account of the feeding of the five thousand, the only miracle that occurs in all four Gospels.[2] Yet, John's gospel alone identifies Jesus as food. Once they've eaten, the crowd talks with Jesus about food. When the people ask for the bread "that gives life to the world," Jesus presents himself as the spiritual food they seek. The identification angers their teachers and rabbis.[3]

## *"I AM the light of the world" (John 8:12)*

Jesus makes this statement during the Jewish Festival of the Booths, or Sukkot, when great lamps lit up the courtyard in front of the Temple at Jerusalem. He presents himself as a light that enlightens the world, just as the lamps lit up the courtyard. The statement comes in the midst of an already acrimonious encounter with the Jewish leaders.

## *"I AM the gate" (John 10:9); "I AM the good shepherd" (John 10:11)*

As he leaves the Temple, where he identified himself as the "light," Jesus runs into a man blind from birth. Since the ancient world regarded such a condition as evidence of sin, not incidence of birth trauma, the disciples ask whether the man's blindness was due to some sin he committed himself or was the fault of his birth

---

2. Matthew 14:13–21, Mark 6:30–56, Luke 9:10–17, John 6:1–15.

3. Genesis 9:3 and 9:6 warn against eating human flesh under any circumstances. No wonder the Jewish leaders were upset.

parents. Jesus dismisses both theories, repeating that he is the light of the world. Mixing mud with spit, he heals the man.

When a crowd gathers, including the man, his parents, neighbors, and Pharisees, the healing story becomes a tiny drama. There's lots of direct speech, but the man who "sees" Jesus most clearly is the blind man. The acuity of his vision shames the Pharisees, leaving them to wonder if they are not blind themselves.

Jesus answers their question indirectly, turning to an even more vulnerable population than the blind: sheep. In the ancient world, sheep had any number of predators, animals and humans. For protection, shepherds penned their sheep at night in stone enclosures that had openings on one side just big enough for the shepherd to lie across. Predators and thieves would first have to reckon with the body of the shepherd. When Jesus identifies himself as the gate, he presumes this practicing of penning sheep. It's a powerful image of protection.

The metaphor intensifies as he identifies himself not just as any shepherd, but a "good shepherd," one who stands ready to block all predators and thieves. This shepherd stands ready to sacrifice his life for the flock's protection.

### *"I AM the resurrection and the life" (John 11:25)*

Jesus identifies himself again at the resurrection of Lazarus. Interestingly, he does this *before* the miracle, not *afterwards*. Before anything happens, who do people think he really is? Lazarus's sister steps up to this challenge, confessing Jesus to be the "Messiah, the Son of God, the one who is coming into the world" (John 11:27). Different from Luke's portrait of a woman "worried and distracted by many things" (Luke 10:41), John's Martha identifies Jesus confidently and accurately as the "Son of God." John makes her one of the first evangelists.

## *"I AM the way, the truth, and the life" (John 14:6); "I AM the vine" (John 15:1)*

Jesus' last meal with his disciples prompts the final two sayings. While the other Gospels tell the story of a last supper, John's account features a final foot washing—and several bruising encounters with his disciples. Both Peter and Thomas demand to know where Jesus is going and why they can't go with him. They want directions, and he tells them he is the only direction they need: "I AM the way." They are left to ponder in silence what it means when one's journey of discipleship ends not in a place, but a person.

This final encounter also features sharp exchanges with the two disciples who will betray Jesus, Peter and Judas. These exchanges prompt another identification, only this time Jesus tells the disciples who *they* are. He calls them "friends" (John 15:14, 15). As friends, they know him; they know his character and his intent. More than knowing intention and character, friends love one another. Jesus charges his disciples to "love one another as I have loved you" (John 15:12).

Betrayal is the sin in friendship. Jesus' identification of his disciples as "friends" foreshadows impending betrayals by both Judas and Peter. In just a few hours, Judas hands over Jesus to be crucified. In just a few hours, Peter denies any association in the least with his friend. Their actions contrast sharply with Jesus' generous declaration of friendship.

In addition to identifying the disciples as "friends," Jesus also identifies them as "branches," while he himself is the "vine." Branches thrive only as long as they stay connected to the vine. Off the vine, they wither and die. This rich metaphor encourages disciples to "stay connected" to the vine. In similar fashion, Jesus repeatedly urges disciples to "abide in me" or "abide in my love" (John 15:5–7, 9), recalling one of the first questions of him: "Where are you staying?" or "Where do you abide?" (John 1:38). Initially, disciples wanted to "abide" with Jesus, but the journey has sorely tested their desire.

## Recognition's Double Edge: Recognizing God, Recognizing Ourselves

Theophany, the visible revelation of God or Mystery, has a double edge of revelation. In the same moment, people suddenly understand who God is and who they are—in their deepest selves.[4]

In 1943 Nazis SS troops deported the author Elie Wiesel and his family to the concentration camp at Buchenwald. In his haunting book, *Night,* the author shares a scene from the internment. Prisoners were forced to watch a mass hanging of other prisoners, one of whom was a thirteen-year-old boy. The boy's weight was not enough to kill him quickly; instead, he slowly strangled. Guards forced the crowd to watch until the boy died. Wiesel heard a man behind him whisper, "Where is God?" Wiesel suddenly realized: "He is hanging here on this gallows."[5] In that moment of revelation, Wiesel knew something about the human condition and something about God.

Encounter fuels all of these identifications of Jesus. The people who prompt these revelations suddenly know something true about themselves. They experience that double edge of revelation. It's entirely appropriate that these "I AM" sayings functioned as the ancient curriculum of the newly baptized. In baptism the newly baptized take on a new identity, "child of God." When they roll around in the post-Easter liturgies, these sayings about Jesus' identity simultaneously reveal the identity of his followers.

## Moses And The First "I AM" Saying

These "I AM" sayings throughout John's gospel would have electrified his audience. Behind them was another theophany: Moses's encounter with God in a burning bush. The encounter reveals something of God and something of Moses as well.

4. Calvin, *The Institutes of the Christian Religion* 1.1.1, 35. "Nearly all the wisdom we possess, that is to say, true and sound wisdom, consists of two parts: the knowledge of God and of ourselves."

5. Wiesel, *Night,* "Segment 4."

The book of Exodus narrates a young man's call from God to lead the Israelites out of Egypt, "out of the land of Egypt, out of the house of bondage" (Exod 20:2). Like every calling, this one clarifies an identity that had been in some flux. People around Moses alternately treat him as a "Hebrew" or as an "Egyptian"; as a "shepherd" or as "a ruler and a judge"; as one of the oppressed, the son of a Hebrew woman and the brother of Miriam, or as one of the oppressors, the adopted son of Pharaoh's daughter. His identity focuses only when he encounters the living God.

The book of Exodus sets up the story. Driven to Egypt by famine in their own land, the Hebrew peoples flourished when Joseph, one of their own, functioned as counselor to the ruler of Egypt. But when "a new king arose over Egypt, who did not know Joseph" (Exod 1:8), the Egyptians enslaved the Israelites, forcing them to build and plant and plow. Seeking to control their numbers, the Pharaoh ordered all young boys to be killed at birth. When the Hebrew midwives resisted, Pharaoh decreed that all male infants drowned in the Nile.

Moses's mother and sister put him in a basket, so that he would not drown. There in the bulrushes, Pharaoh's daughter discovers him, and she resolves to raise him as her own, hiring a Hebrew woman to nurse him. Moses's sister, who has been watching over the infant hidden along the river, knows just the nurse, and Moses's birth mother nurses him before giving him over to Pharaoh's household.

Moses grows up in the royal household but retains enough of his Hebrew identity to kill an Egyptian for mistreating a Hebrew slave. But when he later sees two Hebrew men fighting and intervenes, the men challenge him. They remind him of his royal upbringing: "Who made you a ruler and a judge over us?" (Exod 2:14). Although he is raised Egyptian, Moses identifies with the Hebrew people: yet, his own people refuse to claim him. The rejection echoes Jesus' own, described in the first verses of John's gospel: "He came to what was his own, and his own people did not accept him" (John 1:11).

Fearing for his life, Moses flees into the desert. Even there, he cannot resist intervening in conflict. When he defends the seven daughters of a Midian priest against shepherds who threaten them at a well, the women identify him to their father as "an Egyptian" who helped them (Exod 2:19). Despite his status as an outsider, an "Egyptian" among the Midianites, the priest invites Moses to dine with them, eventually consenting for him to marry one of his daughters, Zipporah.

Although he identifies as Hebrew and looks Egyptian, Moses now marries a Midianite woman. His identity becomes even more mixed. Is Moses a Hebrew, an Egyptian, or a Midianite? To add to the mix, a man raised in a royal household becomes a shepherd, as he tends the flocks of his father-in-law. Once a member of Pharaoh's household, Moses takes up a low-status occupation, becoming a shepherd. When he encounters God in the burning bush, Moses carries a lot of conflicting identities: Egyptian, but also Hebrew; Hebrew, but married to someone outside the twelve tribes of Israel; of royal pedigree, if only by adoption, but doing blue-collar work as a shepherd. It's hard to put this Moses in a box.

The God that Moses encounters erases all ambiguity: "I will send you to Pharaoh to bring my people, the Israelites, out of Egypt" (Exod 3:11). Now Moses has only one identity: liberator. It's not an identity he embraces. He protests his assignment with an impressive array of excuses. The Israelites won't believe him; he's not eloquent; he stutters; his brother Aaron speaks more eloquently. Each time Moses protests, God dismisses the objection. Finally, a man known as "the meekest man on the face of the earth" (Num 12:3) stands down. He embodies the biblical quality of meekness, which is not timidity, but the ability to know when to stand up for something — and when to stand down. Moses accepts his identity as liberator.

But Moses drives a hard bargain. He demands a similar revelation from God. Moses asks God to tell him who sent him, so that he can relay that to Pharaoh. The reply: "Tell them I AM has sent you: I AM who I AM" (Exod 3:14). This is the double edge of theophany. Simultaneously Moses understands who he really is and who God really is. Moses finally recognizes himself; he also recognizes God. Perhaps this revelation, this sheer expression of being, needed no explanation. Perhaps he feels like he has pressed his luck with God far enough, but Moses does not ask the obvious question: "You are—WHAT?!"

The question echoes across the centuries that separate Moses and Jesus. John's gospel picks it up. Here Jesus identifies himself in concrete, embodied, and practical ways, in ways anyone could relate to, but in ways that a good Jew would have immediately recognized as well. The disciples needed it. As the initial chapter of the Gospel makes clear, they're looking for something and someone else.

## Recognizing the Risen Christ: Life in the Resurrection Zone

The disciples had a hard time recognizing Jesus when he was alive. They had an even harder time recognizing the risen Christ. They thought he was a gardener (John 20:15), a ghost (Luke 24:7), a wandering rabbi on the road to Emmaus (Luke 24:13–25); a bossy, backseat driver of a fisherman, someone who preferred to stand on the shoreline and tell other people how to fish (John 21:6); even a short-order cook (John 21:9–14). Clearly, their eyes needed time to adjust. Happily, they get the time they need. The risen Christ doesn't return to his Father right away. He sticks around to establish that death is not the last word. Post-resurrection appearances recorded in each of the Gospel accounts secure that story.

But the risen Christ also returned to spend time with the people he loved. He cooks the disciples breakfast (John 21:9); he breaks bread with them (Luke 24:30); he breathes on them (John 20:22); he opens the Scriptures to them (Luke 24:27); he lets his resurrected body be touched (John 20:27); he gives his followers their marching orders (Matthew 28:18–20).

More important, he forgives them their egregious betrayals by offering them his peace (Luke 24:36, John 19:1ff.) In John's gospel, that peace is given not once, but three times (John 20:19, 21, 26).

Most important of all, this time between resurrection and ascension gives the disciples time to adjust to life in the Resurrection Zone. They needed it.

It's a little like seeing a movie in midday. I remember having an early afternoon meeting cancel right in front of my eyes. I phoned a colleague who was also supposed to be there: "Found time," I said. "Let's go see a movie." That's how we found ourselves in the velvety darkness of an empty movie theater on a weekday afternoon. I don't remember much about the movie, but I do remember moving from the inky blackness of the theater, into the sepia light of the hallway, past the suddenly garish fluorescence of the concession counter, out the front door—and into the dazzling light of a California afternoon. I couldn't see a thing and fumbled for my sunglasses. The transition from darkness to dazzle had been too abrupt. My eyes needed time to adjust.

The same is true of Jesus' original disciples: their eyes needed time to adjust to the light of the world in their midst. Their hearts needed time to recognize the spirit of the risen Christ in their midst.

The inability of the disciples to recognize the risen Christ sends a further message to disciples across the centuries: resurrection is not resuscitation. As much as they may have longed for the familiarity of their master, the disciples don't get the "old Jesus" back again: they get instead the risen Christ. Resurrection signals life on new terms entirely. Then and now, disciples need time to adjust.

## Where's John?

A popular children's series, *Where's Waldo?*, invites children to search for the character in question in a series of minutely detailed illustrations.[6] Waldo wears a distinctive red-and-white–striped

6. British author Martin Handford originally published *Where's Wally?* in the UK. The imprint was picked up in the United States and Canada under the

shirt, a red bobble hat, and black glasses, but he's hard to pick out of scenes packed with objects in a dizzying vertical array. Finding him challenges children and adults to look carefully, exercise discrimination, and recognize Waldo in a sea of competing visual stimuli.

Finding John's gospel in the yearly cycle of readings can be similarly challenging. If your community follows a lectionary, you'll notice that there is no "Year of John." The annual round of prescribed readings marches into Year A with the Gospel according to Matthew. Year B follows, focusing primarily on Mark's gospel. Year C leads with Luke. Then, the three-year cycle circles back to Matthew. No year reckons with John.

John's gospel has not been shortchanged. Rather, readings from the Gospel surface every year in that alleluia-filled Easter season, the Sundays immediately following the celebration of the resurrection. In those fifty days between Easter Sunday and Pentecost Sunday, the Gospel readings focus on the "I AM" sayings from John. And why?

Then and now, these sayings unique to John's gospel address people's deepest needs:

"I AM bread" (John 6:35), because we all know hunger—of body and spirit;

"I AM light" (John 8:12), because we know darkness as the absence of light, as the absence of joy, and as the "dying of the light" or death, that final darkness;

"I AM the gate" (John 10:9), because we know what it's like to be left on the outside;

---

title *Where's Waldo?* The series enjoys enduring popularity, including accompanying workbooks, collections, games, videos, and even an annual 5K run in Colorado Springs. Cf. *The Great Waldo Search* (1989), *Where's Waldo in Hollywood?* (1993), *Where's Waldo? The Wonder Book* (1997), *Where's Waldo? The Great Picture Hunt!* (2006), *Where's Waldo? The Incredible Paper Chase* (2009).

For an example of one of the images: http://4.bp.blogspot.com/-jQ5h9aWHP_c/UZ7KbBWZZKI/AAAAAAAAE2E/nXiCAGiIrPM/s1600/GERMANY.WheresWaldo.jpg.

"I AM the good shepherd" (John 10:11), because we acknowledge that we are all like sheep—the prophet Isaiah (Isa 53:6) was right—and sheep dither;

"I AM the resurrection and the life" (John 11:25), because we all will die, even as we confess that death is not the last word;

"I AM the way, the truth, and the life" (John 14:6), because lies surround us, cheap imitations tempt us, and they pull us off track;

"I AM the vine" (John 15:1), because we remember what it's like to be left out on a limb.

CHAPTER 6

# How I AM Becomes YOU ARE

In his commencement address at Kenyon College in 2005, the late novelist David Foster Wallace assesses life after graduation:

> In the day-to-day trenches of adult life, there is actually no such thing as atheism. There is no such thing as not worshipping. Everybody worships. The only choice we get is *what* to worship. And an outstanding reason for choosing some sort of God or spiritual-type thing to worship—be it J.C. or Allah, be it Yahweh or the Wiccan mother-goddess or the Four Noble Truths or some infrangible set of ethical principles—is that pretty much anything else you worship will eat you alive.[1]

These words would be at home in the world according to John's gospel. The novelist makes several of the same points that the Gospel makes. First, people are hardwired to worship; they can't *not* worship. Atheism is not an option, but merely a dodge for people who don't want to take the trouble to figure out what they *do* worship. Then, some objects of worship are better than others. Some "will eat you alive"; others give life. Finally, as Wallace observes in the beginning of his address, the default setting of the human

---

1. Wallace, *This Is Water*, 98–102. Also http://www.metastatic.org/text/ This%20is%20Water.pdf.

    See also an interview David Foster Wallace did for German television network ZDF: David Foster Wallace, uncut interview, https://www.youtube.com/ watch?v=FkxUYokxH8o.

condition is narcissism, "my deep belief that I am the absolute center of the universe, the realest, most vivid and important person in existence." It takes some heavy spiritual intervention, "some sort of God or spirit-type thing," to rewire that setting.[2]

John's gospel agrees—and offers a remedy. It presents not *something* to worship, but *someone*. This someone is unique, and disciples discover over and over again just who this person is. Repetition is required, because disciples tend to project onto Jesus their own deepest yearnings. Their projections are forms of narcissism.

John's gospel not only tells people who Jesus is, it tells people who *they* are, particularly when they worship this unique *someone*. Worshipping Jesus, disciples become different kinds of people. Jesus' identity powerfully shapes their own, and gradually, they take on the character of the one they worship. John's gospel spells this out. Followers of Jesus become "friends" because they literally know too much: "I have made known to you everything that I have heard from my Father" (John 15:15). Disciples can't pretend ignorance of the larger plan, like a servant, slave, or simple employee. More than mere lackeys, disciples become "branches," because they feed from the life-giving vine that is Jesus. "I AM" becomes "YOU ARE."

In John's gospel, transformation happens through identification.[3] Following Jesus, disciples *become* what they worship. More accurately, disciples become *whom* they worship. The spirit of Jesus, the love of friendship, and the work of forgiveness drive the engine of transformation in John's account. Jesus sends his spirit to dwell in disciples so that they can inspire others. Jesus loves disciples, so that they can love others. Jesus forgives the disciples,

---

2. Ibid., 36.

3. A similar transformation happens in Matthew's gospel, but there blessing transforms identity. In the first public sermon of his ministry, Jesus blesses the unlikely crowd assembled to hear him: "Blessed are the poor in spirit . . . ; blessed are those who mourn . . . ; blessed are meek . . . ." Then, Jesus tells this blessed bunch of people: "You *are* the salt of the earth . . . ; you *are* the light of the world . . . ." (Matt 5:13–14). Blessing transforms them into some of the most valuable commodities in the ancient world. The blessed become a blessing to others.

turning them into forgiven forgivers. Transformation in the Gospel of John doesn't happen magically or overnight. Jesuit theologian and scientist Pierre Teilhard de Chardin captures the pace: "Above all, trust in the slow work of God."[4]

⌒

In this chapter we explore three practices that continue "the slow work of God" into the present: the discernment of spirits, the love of friendship, and the work of forgiveness. How do these practices work transformation today?

## The Discernment of Spirits

"What do you do when you're not swimming?" One of my locker room buddies posed the question. When I told her I taught Christian theology, she paused. "Oh, I'm not at all religious," she responded. "But I *am* a very spiritual person."

There are a lot of spirits out there, and, as Wallace observes, some of them will eat you alive. There's the spirit of consumerism, the spirit of celebrity, the spirit of power and fame and money, the spirit of "keeping up appearances." They lure and tempt and look good, but worshipping these spirits can be costly. How does anyone distinguish among them?

The ancient world cultivated a healthy respect for spirits and an ability to distinguish between good and bad ones. Certain people crossed the border into the spirit world, and Jesus was certainly one of them, along with a host of other miracle workers and rainmakers. Moreover, all of the spirits in the spirit world could identify each other. In Mark's gospel, when Jesus approaches a man "with an unclean spirit," the spirit cries out: "I know who you are, the Holy One of God" (Mark 1:24). The spirit knows precisely who Jesus is, even when disciples do not.

Evil spirits could possess ordinary people, causing fits and creating havoc. Jesus' crowd appeal surged whenever he cast out

4. Teilhard de Chardin, "Patient Trust," 102–3.

an evil spirit, and the Gospels of Matthew, Mark, and Luke recount multiple exorcisms. But the sole spirit that haunts John's gospel is Jesus' own. When Jesus is in the world, his spirit is with him. He tells disciples that when he returns to his Father, he will send his spirit to be with them (John 16:5–7). He wants to make sure they can recognize it. As we have seen, identity matters.

The practice of recognizing Jesus' spirit and distinguishing it from all the other spirits out there is called *discernment*. There's a rich literature on discernment,[5] but John's gospel suggests three distinctive steps: *recognizing* the spirit wherever and in whomever it appears; *asking questions*; then, finally, *test-driving* possible options to see whether they yield desolation or consolation.

## Recognizing the Spirit

Recognizing the spirit requires paying attention. For example, we recognize an apple tree by the fruit it bears. There's no mistaking the fruit. In similar fashion, we recognize the spirit of Jesus by the fruit it bears. The harvest is clear: "The fruit of the Spirit is love, joy, peace, patience, kindness, generosity, faithfulness, gentleness, and self-control" (Gal 5:22). A single "fruit" contains all these good qualities. Finding one guarantees the presence of the others. That means that separating "joy" from "generosity" would be like separating "green" from the tartness of a Granny Smith apple.

We need to nurture these qualities in ourselves and stay close to anyone who radiates them. These people irrigate the soul. A wise spiritual leader has observed: "Good people attract each other like magnets." I smile at the small crowd that always gathers around him in any public setting. He is simply a good person, and we love being in his presence. We hang out with him because he brings out the best in us.

In addition, the insight urges us to attend to how certain people or situations make us feel. Like connective tissue in the body, emotions bind us to particular objects or people. They bridge

5. E.g., Liebert, *The Soul of Discernment* and *The Way of Discernment*; Nouwen, *Discernment*, and Au and Au, *The Discerning Heart*.

between belief and action.[6] Some people always arouse positive emotions, like delight, peacefulness, joy—or at least simple happiness. People who evoke more positive emotions enable us to practice being our best selves. For example, a woman who checks people in at the local YWCA greets everyone with an infectious affection, which they pass on in the locker room.

In a difficult decision or situation, we need to stick with the positive emotions.

## Asking Questions

Three questions help to unpack the work of the spirit: What gives us joy? What are we really good at? Do other people need us to be good at it?[7]

- *What gives us joy?* If joy is an ingredient in the "fruit" of the spirit, it's important to know where to find it. This is a question no one can answer for us, because we alone know what gives us deep and inward delight. Joy differs from happiness, which depends on a wild and crazy array of external factors: diet, the weather, amount of sleep. Joy taps that deeper sense of "fit." We find our joys by digging deep into orienting passions or loves. What ideas or activities do we keep coming back to? What ideas or activities won't leave us alone?

- *What are we really good at?* While I'm the expert in what gives me joy, others have to tell me what I'm really good at. My niece loved to sing; it gave her deep joy. We had to break the news to her gently: she couldn't carry a tune. The news devastated her for a while. Then, the period of mourning ended. She took up piano, her long beautiful fingers always finding the right key. We could easily and truthfully tell her that she was really good at this.

6. Moral theologian William Spohn writes lucidly about the impact of emotion on discernment in his *Go and Do Likewise*, especially chapter 7, "Disposition and Discernment," 142–62.

7. See the video by Fr. Michael Himes, "Three Key Questions." https://www.youtube.com/watch?v=zRGvhe1CKmg.

- *What do other people need from us?* This final question of discernment asks that we take the wisdom gained from the first two questions and look on the world around us. How can we best respond to what the world most deeply needs? When he came into office, Archbishop of El Salvador Oscar Romero (1917–1980) seemed a "safe choice" to both the church and the Salvadoran military. Neither institution reckoned with how the needs of the poor would convert Romero, making him one of their most powerful advocates in Latin America. Assassinated by the military as he celebrated Mass in 1980, he had promised: "I will rise again in the Salvadoran people." Their needs focused his calling.

## Test-Driving Possible Options

Ignatius of Loyola (1491–1556), founder of the Society of Jesus and a master of discernment, advises anyone facing a difficult decision to imagine potential outcomes. Do these outcomes leave one with feelings of desolation or consolation? Consolation gives peace; desolation yields confusion, disorientation, or sadness.

Another master of discernment, Augustine of Hippo (354–430), offers a vivid example. A quintessential "seeker," Augustine chronicles all the ancient philosophies and theologies he test-drove and eventually discarded: rhetoric, an esoteric Gnostic sect, classical philosophy, beauty. The soundtrack for his spiritual autobiography, *Confessions,* could be the old country western song "Looking for Love in All the Wrong Places."[8] Pursuing each of these loves left him only with feelings of emptiness.

Then Augustine discovered a love that had been pursuing him all along. At the beginning of *Confessions,* he captures his quest in words that are still fresh today: "Our hearts are restless until they find their rest in you."[9] Desolation describes the restless

---

8. Check out Johnny Lee's performance of this song: https://www.youtube.com/watch?v=FAyDmJvjxbg.

9. Augustine, *Confessions,* 21.

heart; consolation, the resting heart. Augustine urges disciples to stay with the path of consolation.

## The Love Of Friendship

If you've ever been in love, you long for the beloved to love you in return. In a human calculus, perfect love follows the arithmetic of reciprocal love. Love me as much as I love you. That equals a great relationship.

In the world according to John, though, the math is different. Jesus never tells the disciples to "love me as much as I have loved you." Or even: "Love me just like I've loved you." Like a pen bleeding ink all over the place, divine love leaks. Disciples should let their love be leaky too. Jesus tells them to "love *one another* as I have loved you" (John 13:34, 15:12). Disciples filled with the indwelling spirit of Jesus have work to do. The spirit both enables and requires it.

The work love empowers work is not the warm, fuzzy, sentimental kind of love. It's love with teeth: friendship. John's gospel leaves disciples with powerful new identity. Now, they are friends of God. Accordingly, in a world according to God, they befriend others.

Jesus describes to disciples the radical love of friendship in his final conversation. True to type, encounter prompts the conversation and questions fuel it.

> This is my commandment, that you love one another as I have loved you. No one has greater love than this, to lay down one's life for one's friends. You are my friends if you do what I command you. I do not call you servants any longer, because the servant does not know what the master is doing; but I have called you friends, because I have made known to you everything that I have heard from my Father. (John 15:12–15)

The friendship offered here is both a *knowing* friendship and a *doing* friendship. Both dimensions shape the practice of friendship in the life of discipleship.

## Knowing

"What a friend we have in Jesus . . . ," the old hymn goes. It's great being friends with Jesus, but that friendship is costly. It comes with the weight of *knowing* someone deeply, not just "friending" them on Facebook. As Jesus describes this *knowing* friendship in his final conversation, he compares beings friends with being servants or slaves. The comparison captures people's attention. Servants only know what they're told; they only do what they're told, nothing more and nothing less. More is expected of friends, because they know the intentions, the desires, and the hidden purposes of another. They act accordingly. Compared to servants, friends know too much.[10]

In Jesus' last meal, Jesus calls the disciples his *friends.* He probably senses the nooses of the Roman and Jewish authorities tightening around his neck. His time with his friends is running out. He can't leave them with an operating manual prepping them for every situation they'll encounter after he's gone. He can only remind them of what they already know.

If they'd been more aware of what was going on, the disciples would have protested violently. We can almost hear them: "No, wait! We'd rather be servants, not friends. Just tell us what to do. We don't want to have to think that much about it." It's too hard to "mind" Christ Jesus; it's too dangerous to live in the spirit of friendship, particularly a friendship that's supposed to go out to others. The spirit of that kind of friendship demands paying attention to others. In a letter probably written decades before John's gospel, the Apostle Paul talks to the Philippians about how important it is to act on the basis of what they already know: "be of the same

10. During the first year of my widowhood, a friend across the street phoned me on the first working day after daylight savings had ended. She asked: "I wonder how you're doing. I know how you hate coming home from work in the dark." No one told her what to do; no operating manual for widows existed, much less one with a tab labeled, "On Handling Someone in the Transition from Daylight Savings to Standard Time." Nor had I given her a copy of my anxiety list, even if I could have consciously drawn it up. Like a good friend, she knew me better than I knew myself. She knew instinctively what to do.

*mind*, having the same love, being in full accord and of one *mind*.
. . . Let the same *mind* be in you that was in Christ Jesus" (Phil
2:2–5). Paul can't give them every instruction they might need to
be Christians in the wild and crazy city of Philippi; he can only
urge them to "mind" Christ Jesus. His counsel all boils down to
this: "Remember who loves you; live in that love." The first thing
to notice about Jesus' friendship is that it is a *knowing* friendship.

## Doing

The second dimension of friendship is what friendship with Jesus
*does*. It demands solidarity. Throughout the Synoptic Gospels, Jesus gets censured as "a glutton, a drunkard, a *friend* of tax collectors and sinners" (Matt 11:19; Luke 7:34). According to the Miss
Manners of the ancient world, the people you ate and drank with
were your *friends*, and your *friends* were the people you ate and
drank with. The social equation of friendship was simple: You eat
with certain people; you drink with certain people; therefore, you
are their friend.

In the eyes of his detractors, Jesus ate and drank with all the
*wrong* kinds of people. They're labeled "tax collectors and sinners."
It's worth noting that the two groups didn't get along well with
one another, because anyone who couldn't pay their taxes to the
Temple or to the Romans was judged to be unrighteous, a "sinner." Tax collectors pressured everyone to pay, and their ability
to collect or not collect divided the world between righteous and
unrighteous. Two groups inclined to be enemies came together as
friends around the table Jesus set. They shared a meal. Disciples
do the same.

Shared meals combine both dimensions of friendship, knowing and doing. In this, friendship pushes beyond charity. Charity
sticks with doing—giving money to the poor, giving food to the
hungry, giving drink to the thirsty. Often, the giver remains unknown to the one receiving, an "anonymous" benefactor. In contrast, Jesus dares to be known. Instead of giving money, Jesus walks
with the poor; instead of giving food, he eats with them; instead

of giving water, he turns it into wine—and drinks with them. Jesus invites people into table fellowship with him. Around a common table, they come to know him and one another. Jesus crosses the line from anonymous charity into friendship.

A Berkeley, California parish caught the rhyme of this gesture in their monthly outreach to people experiencing homelessness on the streets. Parishioners spent the afternoon cooking, setting out linens and cloth napkins, the parish china and silverware, and then inviting people off the streets to come and dine. When the meal was ready, they took off their aprons, sitting down with their guests to eat and drink with them. More than offering a meal, they offered friendship. Over time, the parishioners got to know their tablemates, and the guests got to know them. Because they came to know each other's names, guests and parishioners alike gradually understood that they were people worth knowing. That's what happens when people cross the line from charity into friendship.

John's gospel uses friendship as the way to describe the love that characterizes both the love of disciples for God and for each other. When Jesus challenges his disciples to "love one another as I have loved you," he extends his circle of friends to embrace a world that hungers for it. The practice of friendship, combining knowing and doing, meets Jesus' radical challenge.

## The Work Of Forgiveness

In his last days with them, Jesus calls the disciples "friends," inviting them into intimate relationship with him, his Father, and each other. Extending the circle of friendship still further, he challenges them to befriend the world the way he has.

And yet, immediately following that final conversation, the disciples betray him. As we have seen, betrayal is the sin in friendship. With the exception of the "beloved disciple" at the foot of the cross, all of the disciples betray Jesus. As Dietrich Bonhoeffer notes in his classic book, *Discipleship*, Jesus was crucified between two common criminals—not between two of his disciples. In great ways and small, they all betrayed him.[11]

The memory of their betrayal weights heavily on the disciples after Jesus' death. They gather in a locked room after the crucifixion, consumed with fear. They fear running into Jesus as much as they fear running into the Jews or the Romans.

Suddenly, Jesus appears in their midst. The first word to them as the risen Christ is "Peace" (John 20:19). He says it immediately, and he addresses it to their unquiet souls. Then, for emphasis, he says it again: "Peace be with you" (John 20:21). With these words, Jesus unilaterally, unconditionally forgives their fecklessness, their indecision, and their blatant betrayal. This is John's version of Pentecost, the descent of the spirit. Here the spirit descends on a bunch of broken disciples and from a man they'd cruelly betrayed. They have been forgiven.

Only after he's forgiven them, Jesus charges disciples with the ministry of reconciliation. Only after they have been forgiven can they be charged with the task of forgiving others. This is no coincidence. Disciples receive the ministry of reconciliation as *forgiven forgivers*. As they extend reconciliation to others, disciples bear the dangerous memory of their own need for forgiveness and Jesus' ready response.

How do forgiven forgivers practice forgiveness? It's a miracle of grace that forgiveness happens at all. Maybe miracles happen through practice in the sturdy habits of repenting, remembering, and reconciling.[12]

## Repenting

Repentance acknowledges the dark side of the Golden Rule, recognizing and the resisting the nearly irresistible urge to return evil for evil. I steal one of your sheep; you retaliate by wiping out

11. See Bonhoeffer, *Discipleship*, 40, and his chapters on "Retribution" and "The Enemy," 131–45.

12. Cf. Stortz, *A World According to God*, especially "Forgiveness: Healing and Being Healed," 93–111.

my entire flock. I burn down your barn; you go after my house. Violence escalates; retaliations mount; suddenly, entire villages are at war. Each act of retaliation exceeds the originating offense. Violence has become an end in itself.

Repentance, on the part of all parties, victims and offenders alike, stops violence in its tracks. The Greek word for repentance, *metonoia*, literally means "turning away." It signals a turn away from violence on the part of *both* victim and offender.

Too often people treat forgiveness and repentance as if they were separate job descriptions. The offender's task is to repent; the victim's task is to forgive. Christian forgiveness reveals repentance as a task for all, including the victim, as everyone acknowledges a desire for revenge—and resists it.

Repentance confesses the desire for revenge—and then steps away. Repentance on the part of a victim counts as a miracle of grace. Repentance refuses to respond in kind. Forgiveness resists throwing any fuel on the fire, and without more to burn, the fire extinguishes itself.

*Repenting* is the first movement in forgiveness.

## Remembering

A second step in forgiveness overturns the popular counsel to "forgive and forget." The practice of forgiveness is not about forgetting but about remembering. As the disciples moved out into the world, the memory of their own betrayals shaped ministries of compassion. As they forgave others, they had to remember their own deep need for forgiveness. As they remembered their own need for forgiveness, they more readily forgave. Forgiving fused with remembering, and the disciples became forgiven forgivers.

Remembering is important for both offenders and victims. For offenders, remembering guards against reoffending and fuels compassion. For the victim, however, remembering is more difficult. In his work in the Stanford University Forgiveness Project, Frederic Luskin found that remembering on the part of the victim replays injury, magnifying the original offense.[13] Because of this, mediators find the injury seems much greater to the victim than it does to the offender, who tends to minimize what's happened. We've all observed this phenomenon, in small ways and large.

A colleague found that another colleague had publicly put down her work, but never actually confronted her about his disagreement. As she narrated the original offense, I watched her face color and her voice tighten. I could imagine her blood pressure escalating. How could she remember this injury without reinjuring herself? In time, my colleague realized she had a choice. She could choose to remain a victim, harboring the hurt. Or she could choose to move away from victimhood. Even her language changed, as she moved from the accusative to the nominative case: "He hurt *me*" became "*I* want things to change."

Memory works therapeutically in the personal realm. It works restoratively in the public realm. Forgiveness creates "dangerous memory,"[14] because it permits truthful recollection of the past without denying, without reinjuring the victims, and without reviving fresh rage. For example, in the aftermath of apartheid in South Africa, the Truth and Reconciliation Commission chose not to issue broad amnesty. Rather, the Commission would only consider amnesty for those who applied for it with respect to a particular crime and who would agree to speak the truth publicly about what they had experienced. In these public hearings the Commission created a space where citizens could remember. Both victims and offenders needed to confess what had happened.

Only when people truthfully faced the past could they move into a future filled with hope. Bishop Desmond Tutu remarked: "Unless we look the beast in the eye we find it has an uncanny

---

13. Luskin, *Forgive for Good*. See also his website: http://learningtoforgive. com/research/effects-of-group-forgiveness-intervention-on-perceived-stress-state-and-trait-anger-symptoms-of-stress-self-reported-health-and-forgiveness-stanford-forgiveness-project/.

14. The phrase comes from liberation theologian Johannes Metz, *A Passion for God*.

habit of returning to hold us hostage."[15] Memory is the only way to prevent atrocity from happening again.

Going forward into a new future means going back to recover the memory of past injustices. For those who have been injured, this is not easy. Yet the shift gives people another memory to hold alongside the memory of an original violation: the memory of a successful struggle to be a survivor. Like the calcification around a broken bone that forms a bone cast at the break, these memories make people strong at the greatest point of injury.

*Remembering* is a second step in forgiveness.

## Reconciling

Reconciliation is the final step in forgiveness, enabling disciples to embrace that most difficult command of Jesus: "Love your enemies and pray for those who persecute you" (Matthew 5:44). As these words were written, Christians were suffering the first waves of persecution that hit their earliest communities. This command fell hard on disciples facing death.

Commanding love in a time of persecution turned the canons of justice upside down. Yet love is a countercultural stance in a world that threatens to implode in hatred. Forgiveness arrests a cycle of violence and points all parties toward reconciliation.

Note: The "enemy" may still be regarded as "enemy." Jesus did not recommend pretending that the enemy magically morphs into "friend" or "family." My colleague above put the distinction well: "I've forgiven him. That doesn't mean I have to trust him with my life. I'm trying to love him *as an enemy.*"

While respecting the distance that violation creates, Jesus nonetheless pushed for the quality of relationship to alter. "*Love* your enemies and *pray* for those who persecute you." This gesture of defiance comports with everything recorded of Jesus in any of the Gospels. Throughout his earthly ministry, Jesus ministered without discrimination to people in need, many of whom were "enemy" to one another. Rich and poor, Jew and Gentile, woman

15. Tutu, *No Future Without Forgiveness*, 28.

and man, foreigner and native-born, righteous and sinner: Jesus displayed love to all. Perhaps the message he wanted to communicate was simply, "If you travel with me, you cannot afford to have enemies. It will be too confusing to keep track of who they are."

Is forgiveness always possible? Are disciples being asked to do something beyond their human capacities?

The answer to these questions lies in the crucifixion itself. The forces of evil gathered at the foot of the cross, as Jesus hung from a cross, abandoned by friends, followers, even his beloved Father. Yet, his choice was clear. From the cross, Jesus defied evil with a gesture of forgiveness: "Father, forgive them; for they do not know what they are doing" (Luke 23:34).

Christians like to think that Jesus spoke with compassion, but he may well have spit these words out. This man who challenged his disciples to love their enemies did not say: "*I* forgive you . . ." From the cross Jesus summoned a love greater than his own: "*Father*, forgive them . . . ." With these words, he asked God to forgive what he could not.

The forgiveness of Jesus from the cross stands as a stunning example for all disciples. When our powers of reconciliation fall short, we can ask God to forgive our enemies until we can forgive them on our own. C. S. Lewis recalls the cruelty of a schoolmaster who had for years abused his students. Lewis could not forgive him on his own, so he asked God to. Years later, he wrote to his friend Malcolm, "Last week, while at prayer, I suddenly discovered—or felt as if I did—that I had really forgiven someone I have been trying to forgive for over thirty years. Trying, and praying that I might."[16] Over time Lewis found forgiveness; over time forgiveness found him. Reconciliation was possible, even for a grave offense, even with someone who had not asked for it, even for someone long dead.

*Reconciling* is the third step in forgiveness—and recrimination is its chief temptation.

16. Lewis, *Letters to Malcolm*, 106.

## Conclusion

The practices of discernment, love, and forgiveness unbend a heart that has turned in on itself, freeing it for others.

At the end of his commencement address, David Foster Wallace takes his audience on a curious journey. It's not the journey one might expect in a graduation speech. He doesn't escort them to the threshold of a scintillating career, nor does he accompany them to the portal of a whole new chapter in their lives. Rather, he takes them through a "day in the life" of an ordinary person, working an ordinary job, who wants nothing more than to go home, make dinner, and chill out, but remembers there's nothing to eat at home. There's the grocery store, with people moving too slowly and aisles blocked by children. There's the checkout line, packed with tired, ordinary people wanting nothing more than to go home, make dinner, and chill out. There's the traffic on the way home. The scenario is mind-numbingly ordinary and far more likely for a young college graduate than the fast-track corporate world niche the college catalogue hinted at four years ago.

The only choice anyone has is how to think about all of this, and Wallace warns his audience that how they think about it will be determined by what they worship.

> If you worship money and things . . . , then you will never have enough . . . . Worship your own body and beauty and sexual allure and you will always feel ugly, and when time and age start showing, you will die a million deaths before they finally plant you . . . . Worship power—you will feel weak and afraid, and you will need ever more power over others to keep the fear at bay. Worship your intellect, being seen as smart—you will end up feeling stupid, a fraud, always on the verge of being found out.[17]

All of these forms of worship spring from an unconscious narcissism that presents the self as the center of the universe. Freedom *from* self is simultaneously freedom *for* others, as Wallace puts it, "being able truly to care about other people and to sacrifice

17. Wallace, "This Is Water," 7. Also at http://www.metastatic.org/text/This%20is%20Water.pdf.

for them, over and over, in myriad petty little unsexy ways, every day."[18] The practices of discernment, friendship, and forgiveness unbend a heart that has turned in on itself, freeing it for others.

18. Wallace, *This Is Water*, 120.

# Conclusion

A CROSS-COUNTRY ROAD TRIP beckoned. I'd left a position in Berkeley, California, for a new call in Minneapolis. After flirting briefly with the idea of flying there and having the car towed, I decided that I wanted to drive.

I downloaded a map. Maps give spatial location. They place something in relationship to what's around it. Maps identify landmarks. Here's the Great Salt Lake; there are the Rockies. No towns exist along this long stretch of road in Nevada, so make sure the car is gassed and the water bottle full. If I could cover two states and one mountain range each day, I'd make it to Minneapolis in three days.

I also printed out directions. Directions provide a linear sequence of steps that gets you from starting point to destination. This route was simple: "Go 80 mph on Interstate 80 and then turn left at Des Moines."

Finally, I carried a compass just for good measure. A compass registered "true north"; it told me where the sun rose and set. I knew to keep a baseball cap nearby when the route went straight into the rising sun. I knew when I'd catch the glare of the setting sun in my rearview mirror.

Maps, directions, and compass: let the journey begin.

I blasted out of Berkeley early one summer morning. I crossed California and Nevada, summiting the Sierra Nevadas in between. I reached Salt Lake City, Utah, by dusk. The next day I moved through Utah and Colorado, crossing the Rockies. The second night found me in Kearney, Nebraska. The day after that I rolled through the rest of Nebraska and into Iowa, turning north at Des Moines. I sighted the skyline of Minneapolis by late afternoon.

I had driven through rainshowers and sunshowers, rainbows and bursts of hail. I had chatted with truck drivers and other weary travelers. I had watched the land fold up into mountains, then flatten into ancient sea beds and great plains. I had followed the North Platte, home of the Arapaho, Pawnee, and Lakota. It had been an extraordinary journey.

～

Discipleship is also a journey. It's not just an extraordinary journey, it's the journey of a lifetime, one which involves no maps, no directions, and a "true north" no compass can point to. The journey of discipleship is all about *someone*, someone who is himself "true north." That *someone* guides travelers simply by calling them out.

"Follow me." The call begins the journey. And, in John's gospel, the call also concludes the journey. Travelers need to keep hearing those words along the way, because they don't get it right the first time. Distractions abound, delays are common, and simple exhaustion takes over. The good news is that these travelers don't *need* to get it right the first time. To stay on track, they need only to keep listening.

It would be presumptuous of me to tell you what the journey would be like for you. Worse, it would sound preachy. If you're on that journey, you know what I mean. If you're thinking about heading out, you'll find that out. Either way, you'll be grateful I didn't preach at you. But I can tell you what the journey was like for me. What I know is provisional and incomplete. Still, it's not nothing.

"Follow me." The call to discipleship is not specific in the ways that satisfy a traveler—at least not this one. If Jesus had named a *place,* as in "Follow me to Minneapolis," I would have downloaded directions and met him there. A lot of fellow travelers turn discipleship into a place. They spend a lot of ink downloading directions to a destination like heaven or natural and supernatural ends. But for me, discipleship is finally not about getting there.

If Jesus had named a *path*, as in "Follow me along Interstate 80 East," I would have pulled out a map and found the way on my own. A lot of Christians turn discipleship into a path, offering a way to follow or a series of steps to climb. But for me, discipleship is not finally about ascent or self-help.

Let me be honest. As a trained theologian, I've not only watched fellow travelers try to turn discipleship a place or a path, I've done it myself. A wise colleague stated the obvious: "Hey— the manger held a baby, not a Bible—and certainly not a book of confessions."

If God came to humans as a person, then the most important thing to do is get to know God. Think about it. If God came as a Bible, you'd want to know what's in it. If God came as a book of confessions, you'd want to be in compliance. But if God comes as a person, you'd better get to know him. The best way to do that is hang out for a while. The best way to do that is say "yes!" when the person issues an invitation to "follow me."

So, if Christianity is about being in relationship with a God who continues to invite travelers into discipleship today, two critical questions emerge: who is this person, Jesus, the human face of God? And how can we hear the call today?

Those questions animate this book, for in a real sense, every book is its own journey.

Like anyone contemplating such a journey, when exploring this opportunity, I began by checking out the lay of the land. In the first chapter, I dug deeper into John's distinctive way of surveying the terrain of discipleship. I probed the world *behind* the text, the context in which the Gospel was written, examining its cultural, political, ethnic, and religious tensions. I studied how the author of the Gospel creates a world *of* the text, responding to, even resisting those tensions, and how the world *in front of* the text explores the world readers inhabit.

When these worlds come together, key insights emerge. Those direct the rest of the journey: an attention to time, vivid encounters, provocative questions, matters of identity, and practices for keeping on track.

Like anyone contemplating a journey, I then wanted to keep track of time. If the journey moves into a relationship, you mark time by remembering. What you remember are the "firsts": how you first met, where you first traveled together, when you first kissed, when you first knew you were going to spend the rest of your lives together. Remembering strengthens the bond.

John's gospel orients travelers with its own myths of beginning, the birth of the cosmos and the birth of discipleship. Jesus' own words of orientation invite travelers then and now to follow him.

Like anyone contemplating a journey, I also wanted to meet my traveling companions. After all, we were headed in the same direction. Along the way, we'd depend on each other for food, clothing, and good stories.

John's gospel offers vivid traveling companions, probably the most carefully drawn and voluble in any of the Gospels. A lot of them come from communities outside the mainstream of the Roman and Jewish centers of power: a Samaritan woman, a mother (Jesus' own!), a rabbi afraid of his own colleagues, the two unmarried sisters Mary and Martha, a man born blind, and people who worked the lower end of the professional scale, fishermen and shepherds. All these people have conversations with Jesus that leaven the journey.

Like anyone contemplating a journey, I knew I'd have lots of questions—and that questions would be posed to me as well. What are you doing? Where are we going? Have you ever been here before? Questions drive those conversations forward.

John's gospel is driven more by questions than the discourses they prompt. The discourses may attract scholarly speculation, but ordinary disciples simply ask for what they need. Questions open into encounter.

The most pressing questions concern identity: Who are you really? While the other Gospels locate Jesus in terms of a Hellenistic Jewish context, John's Jesus emerges as savior who meets basic human needs for food, water, light, and life. As Jesus identifies himself, he identifies those traveling with him.

Finally, like anyone going on a journey, I want to be prepared. What do I need for the road ahead? And how can I stay on track? When I climbed Kilimanjaro, I pored over guidebooks and gear lists. I knew there were no convenience stores every 1,000 feet.

John's gospel offers a series of practices to help travelers stay together and stay on track. A series of practices supply the relational glue any group of people needs to stick together: discernment, friendship, and forgiveness.

Why does this matter for would-be travelers today? Because humans are quintessentially meaning-seeking creatures. They seek meaning in sacred places. Countless pilgrims journey to Mecca or Jerusalem or Santiago de Compostela or Lumbini, hoping to find in these holy centers a place with heart. They seek meaning in sacred paths, and thousands of self-help books offer to lead the way. Still others seek meaning in a person, and they flock to gurus, guides, and other charismatic figures.

John's gospel offers a God who "flocked to" humans. As the opening lines so elegantly claim, "the Word became flesh and dwelt among us." This person came to hang out in this crazy world and experience the full range of the human condition. In the end, this person left behind nothing more and nothing less than love—and the invitation to keep following.

As they follow, disciples take on the characteristics of the one they follow.

"I AM" becomes "YOU ARE."

Let it be so.

# Bibliography

Au, Wilkie, and Noreen Cannon Au. *The Discerning Heart: Exploring the Christian Path*. Mahwah, NJ: Paulist, 2006.

Auden, W. H. *The Age of Anxiety: A Baroque Eclogue*. Princeton, NJ: Princeton University Press, 2011.

Augustine, *Confessions*. Translated by R. S. Pine-Coffin. New York: Penguin, 1961.

Bass, Diana Butler. *Christianity After Religion: The End of Church and the Birth of a New Spiritual Awakening*. New York: HarperCollins, 2013.

Bonhoeffer, Dietrich. *Discipleship*. Translated by Martin Kuske and Ilse Todt. Minneapolis: Fortress, 2003.

Brown, Raymond E. *The Churches The Apostles Left Behind*. Mahwah, NJ: Paulist, 1984.

———. *The Gospel According to John I-XII*. The Anchor Bible 29. New York: Doubleday, 1966.

———. *The Gospel According to John XII-XXI*. The Anchor Bible 29A. New York: Doubleday, 1970.

———. *The Gospel and Epistles of John: A Concise Commentary*. Collegeville, MN: Liturgical, 1988.

———. *An Introduction to the Gospel of John*. Edited by Francis J. Moloney. New Haven, CT: Yale University Press, 2003.

Bruner, Frederick Dale. *The Gospel of John: A Commentary*. Grand Rapids: Eerdmans, 2012.

Calvin, John. *The Institutes of the Christian Religion*. The Library of Christian Classics 20. Edited by John T. McNeill. Translated by Ford Lewis Battles. Philadelphia: Westminster, 1960.

Culpepper, R. Alan. *Anatomy of the Fourth Gospel: A Study in Literary Design*. Philadelphia: Fortress, 1983.

Dear, John. *The Questions of Jesus*. New York: Image/Doubleday, 2004.

Didion, Joan. *A Year of Magical Thinking*. New York: Alfred A. Knopf, 2005.

Ganss, George E., ed. *Ignatius of Loyola: The Spiritual Exercises and Selected Works*. New York: Paulist, 1991.

Handford, Martin. *Where's Waldo?* Somerville, MA: Candlewick, 2012.

———. *Where's Wally?* London: Walker, 1987.

Lewis, C. S. *Letters to Malcolm: Chiefly on Prayer*. New York: Harcourt Brace, 1992.

Liebert, Elizabeth. *The Soul of Discernment: A Spiritual Practice for Communities and Institutions*. Louisville: Westminster John Knox, 2015.

———. *The Way of Discernment: Spiritual Practices for Decision-Making*. Louisville: Westminster John Knox, 2008.

Luskin, Frederic. *Forgive for Good*. San Francisco: HarperCollins, 2002.

Metz, Johannes. *A Passion for God*. Translated by J. Matthew Ashley. New York: Paulist, 1998.

Neyrey, Jerome. *The Gospel of John in Cultural and Rhetorical Perspective*. Grand Rapids: Eerdmans, 2009.

Nouwen, Henri. *Discernment: Reading the Signs of Daily Life*. New York: HarperCollins, 2013.

Pratt, Mary Louise. *Imperial Eyes: Travel Writing and Transculturation*. London: Routledge, 1992.

Rilke, Rainer Maria. *Letters to a Young Poet*. Translated by M. D. Herter Norton. New York: W. W. Norton, 1993.

Schneiders, Sandra. *The Revelatory Text: Interpreting the New Testament as Sacred Scripture*. Collegeville, MN: Michael Glazier/Liturgical, 1999.

Spohn, William C. *Go and Do Likewise: Jesus and Ethics*. New York: Continuum, 1999.

Stortz, Martha Ellen, *Blessed to Follow: The Beatitudes as a Compass for Discipleship*. Minneapolis: Augsburg Fortress, 2008.

———. *A World According to God: Practices for Putting God at the Center of Your Life*. San Francisco: Jossey-Bass, 2004.

Teilhard de Chardin, Pierre. "Patient Trust." In *Hearts on Fire: Praying with Jesuits*. Edited by Michael Harter, 102–3. Chicago: Loyola, 2005.

Tutu, Desmond Mpilo. *No Future Without Forgiveness*. New York: Doubleday, 1999.

Vermes, Geza. *Jesus the Jew*. Minneapolis: Fortress, 1981.

———. *The Religion of Jesus the Jew*. Minneapolis: Fortress, 1993.

Wallace, David Foster. *This Is Water: Some Thoughts, Delivered on a Significant Occasion, about Living a Compassionate Life*. New York: Little, Brown, 2009.

Wiesel, Elie. *Night*. New York: Farrer, Straus & Giroux, 2006.

# Acknowledgments

IN 2009 COLLEAGUE, FRIEND, and fellow pilgrim Lisa Fullam and I received a Collaborative Research Grant from the Association for Theological Schools to study immersion trips as the post-modern expression of the ancient practice of pilgrimage. We planned to accompany our students on two immersion trips our institutions ran, one in El Salvador and the other in Mexico City. But first we would hike as much of the ancient pilgrimage route to Santiago de Compostela as we could in three weeks.

We proposed walking the questions of John's gospel. There are so many of them, and they propel the narrative forward. We hoped that talking about them would propel us to Santiago. Instead, other questions dominated our conversation. Was that the alarm? Can we stop here? Where should we stay tonight? Isn't it time for a *café con leche?*

We anticipated learning a lot from John's gospel. Instead, we learned a lot from our feet. Still, journey remains a good metaphor for discipleship, particularly as it's displayed in an account that offers such vivid traveling companions as John's does.

Writing a book is its own journey, and I've had some vivid and wise traveling companions. A group of women from Novato, California, offered the earliest opportunity for me to think about this gospel, and their interest proved to me that one didn't have to self-identify as "Christian" to get something out of it. Christian congregations have been my dominant audience: Incarnation Lutheran in Shoreview, Minnesota; St. Michael's in Roseville, Minnesota; United Lutheran in Eugene, Oregon; and Immanuel

Lutheran in Los Altos, California. I'm grateful for the invitation to speak to congregations in the NW Wisconsin, the Northeast Iowa, and Sierra Pacific Synods of the ELCA. Lay schools of theology prodded me to speak simply without "dumbing down," and I thank lively groups at the Stalcup School of the Theology for the Laity at Brite Divinity School, Spirit in the Desert in Carefree, Arizona, and Pacific Lutheran Theology Seminary's summer ReNEW Institute for freeing me from theological jargon.

Educator and spiritual director Diane Millis read the entire manuscript in its early stages, and she gave me counsel and critique that only a fellow traveler can offer. Gerdenio Manuel, SJ, gave me the spiritual and practical direction I sorely needed to complete the manuscript. Theologian at Saint John's School of Theology and Seminary and executive director of the Collegeville Institute Seminars Kathleen Cahalan offered guidance and wise counsel. I thank her along with all of my colleagues in the Collegeville Institute Seminar on Vocation and the Professions—Bill Sullivan, Doug Schuurman, Rev. Kathy George, John Lewis, and Laura Fanucci. I owe Nancy Ashmore of AshmoreInk my deepest thanks for her literary aesthetic, her editorial expertise, and her allergy to jargon.

To these and so many other companions along the way, I give profound thanks. It's been a great trip—and the journey continues. I end with the words of encouragement medieval pilgrims offered to one another as they made their way to Santiago de Compostela:

Onward and upward! *Ultreya e suseya!*